Lean Execution

THE BASIC IMPLEMENTATION GUIDE FOR MAXIMIZING PROCESS PERFORMANCE

Lean Execution

THE BASIC IMPLEMENTATION GUIDE FOR MAXIMIZING PROCESS PERFORMANCE

Clifford Fiore

CRC Press
Taylor & Francis Group
Boca Raton London New York

CRC Press is an imprint of the
Taylor & Francis Group, an **informa** business

A PRODUCTIVITY PRESS BOOK

CRC Press
Taylor & Francis Group
6000 Broken Sound Parkway NW, Suite 300
Boca Raton, FL 33487-2742

© 2016 by Clifford Fiore
CRC Press is an imprint of Taylor & Francis Group, an Informa business

No claim to original U.S. Government works

Printed on acid-free paper
Version Date: 20160303

International Standard Book Number-13: 978-1-4987-5274-9 (Paperback)

This book contains information obtained from authentic and highly regarded sources. Reasonable efforts have been made to publish reliable data and information, but the author and publisher cannot assume responsibility for the validity of all materials or the consequences of their use. The authors and publishers have attempted to trace the copyright holders of all material reproduced in this publication and apologize to copyright holders if permission to publish in this form has not been obtained. If any copyright material has not been acknowledged please write and let us know so we may rectify in any future reprint.

Except as permitted under U.S. Copyright Law, no part of this book may be reprinted, reproduced, transmitted, or utilized in any form by any electronic, mechanical, or other means, now known or hereafter invented, including photocopying, microfilming, and recording, or in any information storage or retrieval system, without written permission from the publishers.

For permission to photocopy or use material electronically from this work, please access www.copyright.com (http://www.copyright.com/) or contact the Copyright Clearance Center, Inc. (CCC), 222 Rosewood Drive, Danvers, MA 01923 978-750-8400. CCC is a not-for-profit organization that provides licenses and registration for a variety of users. For organizations that have been granted a photocopy license by the CCC, a separate system of payment has been arranged.

Trademark Notice: Product or corporate names may be trademarks or registered trademarks, and are used only for identification and explanation without intent to infringe.

Library of Congress Cataloging-in-Publication Data

Names: Fiore, Clifford, 1960- author.
Title: Lean execution : the basic implementation guide for maximizing process performance / Clifford Fiore.
Description: 1 Edition. | Boca Raton : CRC Press, 2016. | Includes bibliographical references and index.
Identifiers: LCCN 2015039853 | ISBN 9781498752749
Subjects: LCSH: Lean manufacturing. | Six sigma (Quality control standard)
Classification: LCC HD58.9 .F56 2016 | DDC 658.4/013--dc23
LC record available at http://lccn.loc.gov/2015039853

Visit the Taylor & Francis Web site at
http://www.taylorandfrancis.com

and the CRC Press Web site at
http://www.crcpress.com

Contents

Preface ix

SECTION I   LEAN BASICS

1   Lean Fundamentals 3
   1.1   Lean or Six Sigma? 3
   1.2   Lean History 5
   1.3   Lean Definition 6
   1.4   Flow 7
   1.5   Customer Value 7
   1.6   Waste Categories 8
   1.7   Push versus Pull Systems 9

2   Value Streams and Value Stream Mapping 11
   2.1   Defining a Value Stream 11
   2.2   Mapping Considerations 12
   2.3   Process Considerations for Value Stream Mapping 15

SECTION II   LEAN ASSESSMENT

3   Lean Baseline Assessment 21
   3.1   Baseline Definition 21
   3.2   Baseline Overview 21
   3.3   Baseline Success Factors 23
   3.4   Baseline Execution 28

4   Product Analysis 43
   4.1   Product Analysis Overview 43
   4.2   Time-Value Chart 45
   4.3   Spaghetti Diagram 46
   4.4   Communicating with Tools 47

5 Operator Analysis 49
- 5.1 Operator Analysis Overview 49
- 5.2 Takt Time 51
- 5.3 Line Balancing: The Problem 52
- 5.4 Bottlenecks 53
- 5.5 Garden Hose Analogy 53
- 5.6 Line Balancing: The Solution 55
- 5.7 Operator Process Variation 56
- 5.8 Ergonomics 58

6 Machine Analysis 61
- 6.1 Machine Analysis Overview 61
- 6.2 Overall Equipment Effectiveness 61

SECTION III LEAN IMPROVEMENT

7 Five S 67
- 7.1 5S Overview 67
- 7.2 5S Implementation 68

8 Standard Work 71
- 8.1 Defining Standard Work 71
- 8.2 Standard Work Tools 73
- 8.3 Adjusting Standard Work 74

9 Cell Design 79
- 9.1 Cell Definition 79
- 9.2 Visual Systems 80
- 9.3 Group Technology 81

10 Process Improvement Enablers: Setup Reduction, Total Productive Maintenance, and Mistake-Proofing 85
- 10.1 Setup Reduction 85
- 10.2 Total Productive Maintenance 87
- 10.3 Mistake-Proofing 88

11 Materials Management 91
- 11.1 Materials Management Overview 91
- 11.2 Kanbans 92
- 11.3 Little's Law 94

12	**Knowledge Management**	**97**
	12.1 Knowledge Management Overview	97
	12.2 Knowledge Management System	98
13	**General Guidelines for Lean Implementation**	**101**
	13.1 Lean Perspective	101
	13.2 General Guidelines	101
	13.3 Lean Principles	104

Appendix A: Using Six Sigma to Improve Product Quality **107**

Appendix B: Forms and Worksheets **109**

Appendix C: Glossary **121**

Appendix D: Answers **125**

References **133**

Index **135**

About the Author **143**

Preface

If someone had told me, as I was about to embark on my first job approximately 30 years ago, that one day I would write a book about Lean (actually, any book for that matter), that is a bet that I would have wholeheartedly taken—and lost. So, here we are, 30 years later, and *Lean Execution: The Basic Implementation Guide for Maximizing Process Performance* is not the first book that I have written about Lean, but the third!

My career started in a pretty typical fashion for a newly graduated engineering wannabe. During the first few years of my career, I was afforded the opportunity to migrate to different jobs and gained experience in manufacturing, production support, design, and engineering. About eight years into my career, I was given the opportunity to participate in a week-long Lean training class. Having previously participated in similar training sessions, I wore the battle scars of other initiatives that had come and quickly disappeared. Based on this, my expectations for the Lean training were not very high, even though at the time, I had no idea what *Lean* was or what it could mean for a business.

Given my engineering mentality, I was expecting the Lean instructor to attempt to dazzle us with fancy tools and techniques. My thought pattern was, if it's not difficult and complex, it can't be any good.

As the training progressed, and as module after module was completed, I found myself repeating the same thoughts in my head over and over: "Is that it?," "That's too simple," and "It's just common sense." However, the more I thought about the concepts and methods that were presented, the more I began to appreciate the power and pure simplicity of Lean. Even now, on the very first day of teaching classes about Lean, I will invariably blurt out, "Lean is not rocket science," because, truly, it is not. Lean tools are very straightforward and easy to understand and apply. They go to the heart of addressing the basic fundamentals that every organization needs to have in place.

Looking back on the experience now, attending that week-long training class turned out to be a seminal moment in my career. Having gained first-hand exposure and an appreciation for the Lean methodology, I was ultimately able to steer my career in the direction of being able to be directly involved with implementing Lean concepts. It has been a rewarding journey, and I have never looked back.

The current Lean movement has been underway for more than 20 years. During this time, the Lean community has steadily grown with applications of Lean extending well beyond the factory floor. As a by-product of this implementation, many excellent books have been written on the subject of Lean. *Lean Execution: The Basic Implementation Guide for Maximizing Process Performance* was written with the goal of adding to this body of knowledge.

The focus of this book highlights Lean methods and tools that can be implemented to maximize process performance. These methods and tools are introduced and explained, but the emphasis of this book is on the guidelines, process conditions, and tips to ensure success from Lean implementation. For example, there are many books on the market that explain how to construct a value stream map, but few that explain the process conditions and characteristics that are necessary to ensure that a value stream map can be completed successfully.

This book is the culmination of thoughts and experiences from firsthand implementation of Lean tools and methods. The insights shared in this book were acquired through trial and error. From a personal perspective, applying Lean tools correctly is certainly important, but the most critical element is to understand the big picture regarding when to use the tools and what understanding can be gained from their application.

The ability of Lean practitioners to ask questions is their most important virtue. Tools are merely the mechanisms to be used to answer questions and gain insight about a process. Undoubtedly, the answers acquired will lead to more questions. In this respect, executing Lean and applying the tools are essentially a journey on the continuum of knowledge gathering and learning.

The ability to see the big picture, ask questions, and apply the correct tools in the right way to learn and gain insight about the process represent the skills that I hope for every Lean practitioner to possess. This is the message I hope to convey and the reason why this book was written.

I sincerely hope that you enjoy *Lean Execution: The Basic Implementation Guide for Maximizing Process Performance* and that it assists you with your own Lean journey!

Clifford Fiore

LEAN BASICS   I

Section I presents Lean fundamentals and reviews value streams and value stream mapping.

Chapter 1

Lean Fundamentals

1.1 Lean or Six Sigma?

The pressure placed on companies to improve performance is more intense now than it has ever been. With the fierce competition that exists in the current business environment, the key discriminator for the most successful companies is the ability to provide a continual stream of high-quality, low-cost products that reach the customers faster than their competitors.

For many companies, the adoption of a philosophy of continuous improvement has been the recipe for success. The relentless pursuit to maximize efficiencies using Lean and Six Sigma techniques has been instrumental in this improvement. But, for practitioners looking to engage in continuous improvement activities, deciding whether to use Lean or Six Sigma can be a daunting question. The answer to the question (and I am sure you guessed it) is a resounding "It depends!"

More precisely, it depends on the goals of the organization and the areas in which it wants to improve. In nearly all instances, improvement opportunities can be summarized into three key areas: (1) cycle time, (2) cost, and (3) quality.

When we consider the use of Lean and Six Sigma methodologies to make improvements in these areas, they are distinctly different, but complementary. In other words, it is imperative that the correct methodology be employed in order to achieve the desired goal.

Let us take a closer look at the characteristics of Lean and Six Sigma and see how these methodologies align with the improvement opportunities. Lean is about eliminating waste (non-value-added activities), standardizing work processes, and achieving *flow*. By eliminating unnecessary tasks, it is logical to assume that it will take less time and resources to complete the finished product. Consequently, the key benefit in the application of Lean is a reduction in cycle time.

By their very nature, Lean projects possess characteristics that tend to be *process-centric*. Typically, emphasis is placed on examining value streams and work processes, as opposed to focusing on individual products. The Lean tool set provides rigor in assessing the activities of the product (the "thing" going through the process*), the operators, and even the machines (if applicable) employed by the process. Through successful adaptation of these tools, improvement in the overall process can be achieved.

Six Sigma is focused on variation reduction and process control. The Six Sigma approach is based on a simple premise: in order to achieve a consistent and predictable output, it is necessary to control the inputs. Often, this statement is expressed as the mathematical expression $y = f(x)$.

The Six Sigma methodology employs a suite of statistical tools to understand the degree, as well as the sources, of variation. Projects under the Six Sigma umbrella tend to be *product-centric*. For example, a product with a high scrap rate would employ Six Sigma tools to identify the contributing factors that cause the non-conformities. Once a solution had been identified and implemented, Six Sigma tools would also be used to ensure that the activities for producing the product had adequate controls in place for maintaining the improved level of performance.

The fuel that makes the Six Sigma engine go is data. Access, and the analysis of data, is the key for the successful utilization of a Six Sigma program—and a Design for Six Sigma program for that matter as well. The ability to identify and analyze the causes of variation are the keys to the Six Sigma approach. Consequently, the primary benefit in the application of Six Sigma is a reduction in quality defects.

It is important to recognize that although we highlighted benefits related to cycle time and quality in our review of Lean and Six Sigma, cost is not forgotten. Significant cost benefits can be realized from the application of both Lean and Six Sigma. For example, for a Lean project, cost benefits can be realized from reduced labor and resources required to produce a product. Likewise, reduced scrap rates and higher product yields from a Six Sigma project would translate into significant cost savings as well.

---

* The thing going through the process does not need to be a physical product. In non-factory and administrative-type processes, the thing going through the process is information.

It is also important to note that the benefits highlighted for Lean and Six Sigma are not mutually exclusive. For example, the ability to standardize a work process in a Lean project provides the by-product of reducing the variation that exists in the process. In the Six Sigma world, the ability to eliminate a chronic rework cycle, for example, would certainly improve the cycle time for producing the product.

Many companies that utilize both Lean and Six Sigma methodologies have adopted the term *LeanSigma* and formally applied it in the naming of their continuous improvement organizations (George 2002, p. 93). Regardless of the organizational structure, the bottom line is this: companies that understand the fundamental differences in Lean and Six Sigma, and recognize the complementary nature of these methodologies in achieving benefits related to cycle time, cost, and quality, are the ones that will gain the most from its implementation.

This book is focused on the application of the Lean methodology. The material is organized into three sections: (1) Lean overview and a review of Lean fundamentals, (2) assessment tools to review the current state and baseline level of process performance, and (3) techniques and methods for developing a Lean process. End-of-the-chapter questions and problems are provided to enable readers to test their knowledge of the key learning points.

1.2 Lean History

The current Lean movement underway in the United States began to take hold in the mid-1990s.* However, the elements of Lean, and concepts that are still in place even today, can trace its roots back well over 100 years.

The late nineteenth century was characterized pre-dominately by craft manufacturing. Products were made in accordance with customer specifications, but each product was unique. Product quality was highly variable, and production quantities were extremely low with little inventory.

Manufacturing began to change at the turn of the twentieth century. The adoption of the assembly line by Henry Ford allowed mass production to

---

* The Lean movement was preceded by a focus on Six Sigma, and an earlier continuous improvement movement in the mid-1980s focused on total quality management and total quality leadership.

become a reality. Interestingly, Ford did not invent the assembly line. That distinction goes to Ransom Olds (Domm 2009, p. 28).

In many respects, Ford was a Lean proponent. Utilization of the assembly line that paved the way for mass production resulted in dramatic reductions in product cost, improved quality that enabled interchangeable parts, and increased worker wages. Standardization in work practices and products took hold, along with concepts to eliminate waste. Practices around motion and time studies were adopted. However, issues with labor strife also emerged during this period related to worker stress, boredom from performing the same repetitive tasks day in and day out, and operator safety.

The Lean production system currently employed evolved during the post-World War II period and has been popularized, most notably, by Toyota. This system represents a hybrid of the previous craft and mass production systems by combining characteristics of both. The current Lean model strives to achieve high product quality, low inventory with small batch sizes, short cycle times for varied product selections, and employ an engaged workforce (Spear and Bowen 1999, p. 96).

1.3 Lean Definition

If you look in Merriam-Webster's Collegiate Dictionary (2007), the definition of *Lean* is something that contains little fat, or something that is severely curtailed or reduced. Translating this definition to the business world, Lean means:

> *Producing what is needed, when it is needed, with the minimum amount of materials, equipment, labor, and space.*

The term *Lean*, as applied in this context, is credited to John Krafcik, who coined the term while working as a graduate student at the Massachusetts Institute of Technology (Krafcik 1988, p. 41).

So what is the objective of a company that wants to be Lean and employ a Lean process? Essentially, the goal for a company adopting the Lean philosophy is to make each process as efficient and effective as possible, and then to connect those processes in a stream or continuous chain focused on flow and maximizing customer value.

What do we mean by the terms *flow* and *customer value*? Let us examine each one in more detail.

1.4 Flow

Everyone can relate to the concept of flow if we use the example of water flowing continuously through a stream or river. Similar to this example, flow in the business world refers to the continuous movement of products and information through various processes to create a product. The goal here is to minimize idle time between all of the processes, which represents inefficiency and waste.

The elimination of waste is a key tenet of Lean. It is the basis upon which companies can improve productivity and maximize customer value.

1.5 Customer Value

Simply stated, customer value refers to specific activities that add value to the products and services that customers buy. The determination of what adds value is made from the customer's—not the company's—perspective.

Under the Lean philosophy, for an activity to be value-added, it must meet the following three criteria:

1. The customer must be willing to pay for the activity.
2. The part or object must change. (Note: for non-factory processes, the second criterion is that the activity must add to the company's knowledge base.)
3. It must be done right the first time.

For an activity to be considered value-added, all three criteria must be satisfied. Any action that does not meet all the three criteria is considered a non-value-added activity and represents waste.

So what are some examples of activities that do not meet the three criteria for a value-added activity? Consider the following:

- Moving parts from one machine to another
- Testing and inspection operations
- Rework and repair activities
- Parts in queue sitting next to a machine
- Sign-offs and approvals
- Attending meetings

All of these activities are examples of waste and do not meet all three criteria. Obviously, the list of non-value-added tasks can be infinitely longer, but the point here to highlight is the magnitude of common, everyday activities performed on a daily basis that do not meet the criteria of adding value to an organization. To put this in perspective, in a typical value stream, the percentage of non-value-added time is greater than 90% of the total time! Stated another way, in most value streams, less than 10% of the total time is devoted to performing value-added activities.

1.6 Waste Categories

So should the goal of an organization be to eliminate all wasteful activities from their processes? While this may be a desired goal, it is not a practical one. There are many conditions that preclude the elimination of certain activities from processes, even if they are classified as non-value-added. For instance, government regulations require that specific levels of oversight and inspection be performed in industries where health or human safety is involved. For example, if, at some point in your life you need a pacemaker (and I hope you never do), wouldn't you insist that the device go through a rigorous testing and inspection process to ensure it is functioning properly before you receive it? Pacemaker manufacturers currently do this, not only because of government regulations, but also because the risk of a product failure can have catastrophic consequences for the customers (the patient in this case), as well as the company.

Waste activities can be classified into any one of seven different categories (Ohno 1988, p. 129). The categories are defined as follows:

1. Defects
2. Overproduction
3. Transportation
4. Waiting (product)
5. Inventory
6. Motion (operator)
7. Processing (unnecessary process steps)

The acronym DOTWIMP, representing the first letter of each of the categories, is often used by Lean practitioners to refer to waste.

Identifying and eliminating waste are the key enabler to maximizing customer value and establishing flow. Once accomplished, a company is well on its way toward transforming itself into a Lean enterprise.

Now that we have defined it, what methods can we employ to identify waste in processes we utilize? The answer to this question leads to a review of production systems and value streams.

1.7 Push versus Pull Systems

The ability to engage a company's value stream is in response to meeting a customer demand. There are two distinct approaches in the way value stream engagement takes place. These are referred to as *push* and *pull* systems.

In a push system, a pre-determined quantity of work is scheduled into the production process. This work quantity is often derived from sales estimates and forecasts. The engagement of the value stream is initiated with adequate lead time to allow for production and delivery. In addition, this system is typically characterized by large batch sizes and, historically, the model that many companies have employed for decades.

In a pull system, the value stream is engaged in direct response to customer demand. Materials to be used in the process are staged at the point of consumption. As materials are consumed, signals are sent to previous steps in the process to pull forward sufficient quantities to replenish those that have been consumed. Many pull systems are made-to-order systems that employ small batch sizes. The pull system is representative of a Lean approach with correspondingly low levels of work-in-process inventory (Wilson 2010, p. 138).

Simple examples from the fast-food industry can be used to contrast the differences in push and pull systems. Pre-made food sitting under warming lamps waiting to be purchased is an example of a production model engaged in a push system. In this case, the food is prepared by the company in anticipation of being able to sell it, and done so independent of any customer order. In this model, the value stream for preparing the food is initiated at the sole discretion of the company. This approach poses some inherent risk, since there is no guarantee that the product will be sold before its shelf-life expires.

Conversely, an example of a pull system is the production model that is employed by numerous submarine sandwich companies. With this approach, a sandwich is made in direct response to a customer order. This affords the product to be customized and tailored to meet very specific customer specifications. In this case, the value stream for preparing the sandwich is not engaged until the customer order is placed. Consequently, in this model, there is no finished goods inventory, so the potential risk of needing to discard pre-made sandwiches is eliminated.

QUESTIONS

1. What are the characteristics of Lean and Six Sigma projects?
2. Describe the typical levels of quality, production quantities, and inventory for a craft manufacturing process.
3. What benefits resulted from the increased utilization of the assembly line?
4. What were some of the issues that resulted from the emergence of mass production?
5. What are the goals of a Lean production system?
6. What is the definition of *Lean* as it relates to a business process?
7. What is the definition of *flow* for a Lean system?
8. What are the three criteria that define a value-added activity?
9. The determination of added value is made from what perspective?
10. List the seven categories of waste. What acronym are they known by?
11. Generally speaking, what percentage of time in a typical value stream is value-added?
12. Compare the differences in push and pull systems.

Chapter 2

Value Streams and Value Stream Mapping

2.1 Defining a Value Stream

Simply stated, a value stream represents all of the activities, materials, people, and information that must flow and come together to provide and deliver value (product or service) that the customer seeks. In reality, a value stream both starts and ends with the customer. Customers define the value they seek in terms of the products or services they desire. Companies engage their internal value streams to provide the goods or service to satisfy their customer's needs. The value stream ends, and comes full circle, upon the delivery of the product or service to the customer.

The ability to document a value stream, using a process known as value stream mapping, is a key activity to fundamentally understand what is really going on in a process. If we truly understand the current level of performance across all aspects of the process, we can then identify specific elements of the process that are underperforming and require improvement. These objectives—the ability to assess the current state of performance and identify opportunities for improvement—are the primary reasons for creating a value stream map.

An important aspect of the value stream mapping effort is to document the process from firsthand observation, as opposed to merely referring to work instructions or documented procedures that may be in place. The reason for this is that in many instances, the actual process being performed has evolved over time and deviates from formalized procedures that may have been established some time ago. The term *hidden factory* is used to identify the actions and activities for what is actually taking place in a process, as opposed to documented work instructions that do not represent reality.*

2.2 Mapping Considerations

A number of considerations need to be taken into account to maximize the benefits from the mapping exercise. The first consideration is the scale and scope of the process under examination. For example, imagine that you work for a company and are assigned the task of creating a value stream map for product XYZ, a product with a historically high manufacturing cost. What should the starting point be for documenting the process? Should it begin with the first machining operation, or maybe earlier in the process when the raw materials are requisitioned? Likewise, should the final step be the last machining operation, or possibly later in the process when the final inspection occurs? Should the map extend beyond the company's walls and include activities of suppliers and customers?

Existing information and insight about the process can be the guidepost in answering these questions. For example, are metrics or data available reflecting current process performance or information that provides insight regarding problem areas that are currently being experienced? Obviously, the more information that is known, the more focused the map can be in documenting a specific aspect of a process.

As a general rule, however, a value stream map is intended to be a macro-level view of a process. Since the mapping activity is quite often the first step in assessing a process, it is imperative to take a high-level perspective in order to avoid missing a potential opportunity for improvement. To support this, as a general guideline, it is recommended that the initial value stream map of a process specify between 4 and 10 steps.

Based on the information gleaned from the initial map, it may be appropriate to consider a second map to "deep-dive" a specific aspect of the process. For example, let's say that for a first-cut value stream map, the third process step appears to be a problem area. To investigate this further, one option would be to create a second value stream map centered specifically

---

* The activity of value stream mapping is sometimes referred to as a task to document reality. The implication of this term is to address any hidden factory issues that may exist in the process.

on the activities of the third process step. In other words, we could create a new map by identifying and documenting the lower-level details that are associated with the third process step activity. This approach of "peeling the onion layer by layer" is an effective way to drill down and perform deep-dive assessments for specific process areas.

In the following chapters, we will introduce additional tools to further interrogate the initial opportunities identified by a value stream map. Given the nature of this approach, it is not uncommon for a value stream map to identify multiple opportunities for potential improvement. In this respect, a value stream map can be thought of as representing a "blueprint" for instituting a series of improvements within a process.

Figure 2.1 provides an example of a typical value stream map (George et al. 2005, p. 45). Unlike a traditional process map that merely documents specific tasks or activities, a value stream map documents information flows in addition to product flows. In Figure 2.1, this is denoted as the forecast, ordering, and scheduling activities that are displayed in the top portion of the map. As an added supplement, data can be captured and linked with each process step to convey a more complete picture of the process under

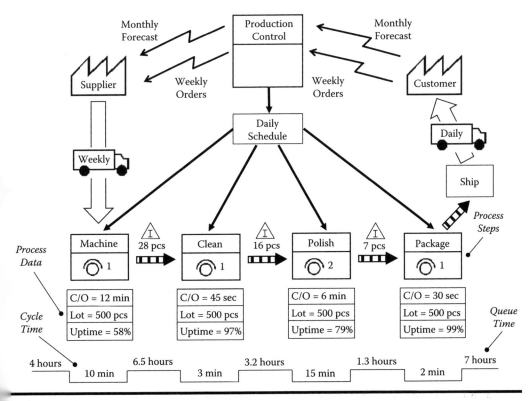

Figure 2.1 Value stream map example.

14 ▪ *Lean Execution*

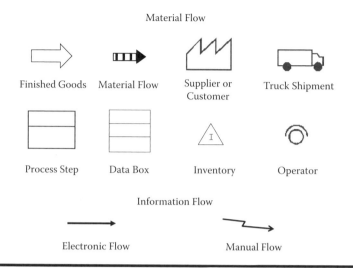

Figure 2.2 Value stream map symbols.

review. As shown in Figure 2.1, the changeover (C/O) time, lot quantity, and uptime are displayed for each step.

Aligned to the process steps, and referenced on the stepped scale below the process step blocks as shown in the figure, are the corresponding cycle times. Queue times are also referenced on the stepped scale as the designated times between the process steps. In addition, a work-in-process inventory is documented on the map, with product quantities noted alongside the inventory symbol (the capital "I" in a triangle). Figure 2.2 provides a companion listing and description of the symbols used in Figure 2.1 (George et al. 2005, p. 49).*

A key take-away from a value stream map is a comparison of throughput time versus processing time. Throughput time is defined as the total time that it takes the process to complete a product or service. It is the sum total of the processing time for all process steps plus all of the queue time in the process. For the example shown in Figure 2.1, the throughput time is 22.5 hours.

Cycle time, as shown in Figure 2.1, is the total time to complete one part for one process step. Processing time, therefore, is the aggregate total of all individual cycle times for the process. Stated another way, processing time is calculated as the throughput time minus the total queue time in the process:

$$\text{Processing Time} = \text{Throughput Time} - \text{Total Queue Time}$$

---

* Beyond the symbols used in this example, there are other universally recognized value stream map symbols that are available.

In Figure 2.1, the processing time is 30 minutes (0.5 hour). Continuing with this example, we now have calculated values for both the throughput time (22.5 hours) and processing time (0.5 hour). At this point, a logical question to ask is why it takes the part takes 22.5 hours to go through the factory when only a half hour of processing is required.

By comparing throughput time to processing time, we essentially isolate the queue time in the process. This is a key benefit provided by a value stream map. As we highlighted in Chapter 1, queue time is waste* and represents a prime opportunity for reduction or elimination.

As noted in Section 2.1, and a point worth repeating, is that all data referenced on a value stream map should be obtained from firsthand observation. This is accomplished by "walking the process" and documenting the information in real time. To further facilitate this, Lean practitioners advocate creating hand-drawn maps using pencil and paper, as opposed to generating fancy maps that are made using a computer. The book *Learning to See: Value Stream Mapping to Create Value and Eliminate MUDA* (2003), by Rother and Shook, is recognized as the leading how-to guide in value stream mapping practices.

2.3 Process Considerations for Value Stream Mapping

Lean practitioners will undoubtedly tell you that value stream mapping is one of the most important Lean activities. As just described in Sections 2.1 and 2.2, it is a very effective tool in assessing the current state of a process and identifying opportunities for improvement. However, the ability to create an effective value stream map is based on the ability to observe the process. What if this is not possible?

Historically, many companies started their Lean implementation by focusing on the factory. Factory processes possess certain characteristics that make them very conducive to a value stream mapping exercise. Generally speaking, individual process steps within a manufacturing operation can often be completed in a matter of minutes—and in many instances, within a number of seconds. In a mass production–type environment where the value stream is engaged on a regular or even continual basis, the ability to walk the process and perform the firsthand observation is very

---

* As stated in Chapter 1, the "W" in DOTWIMP represents waste.

accommodating. Additionally, in this environment, process steps are highly repeatable and can be witnessed through multiple cycles, thereby enabling the task of documenting the process activity a straightforward proposition. In summary, these characteristics, process steps with short durations, access to observe the value stream when needed, and highly repeatable process steps make the task of completing a value stream mapping for factory processes a fruitful activity.

Many companies, however, beyond the initial factory implementation, have looked to apply the Lean methodology to other parts of their business. The ability to apply Lean in administrative and other transactional processes, specifically as it relates to value stream mapping, poses some interesting challenges. For example, consider a value stream for product development. Individual process steps within the product development process, such as the detail design activity or analytical analysis, often cannot be completed within minutes, and many times can take hours. The frequency that the value stream is engaged may be quite low (for example, how often does Boeing design a new airplane?), thereby limiting the opportunity to "walk the process". In addition, product development projects, even within a specific product area, can vary greatly in size and scope. Consequently, there is the potential for a high degree of variability in the actions and steps necessary to complete the project. These factors often have a similar effect in other administrative-type processes such as purchasing, order replenishment, customer support, and others. To summarize, long cycle times, the frequency of value stream engagement, and high variability of the process steps can limit the ability to effectively complete a value stream map in administrative and transactional-type processes.

So what is the alternative to identify the current-state performance and identify opportunities for improvement for processes where a value stream map cannot be completed? The answer, to remedy the shortcomings of value stream mapping in these instances, is to conduct a Lean baseline assessment.

QUESTIONS

1. What is a value stream?
2. The value stream starts and ends with whom?
3. What is the purpose of value stream mapping?
4. What does the term *hidden factory* mean?

5. What is the guideline for the number of process steps to include for a first-cut value stream map?
6. Is a value stream map intended to depict a high-level or detailed view of a process?

    Refer to the following excerpt of a value stream map to answer questions 7–10:

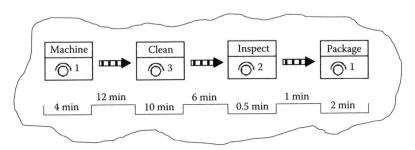

7. What is the total processing time for the four-step process?
8. What is the throughput time for the four-step process?
9. How many operators are required for the inspection step?
10. What is the queue time for the cleaning operation?
11. A manufacturing process has a processing time of 12.7 minutes and a queue time of 58.5 minutes. What is the throughput time for this process?
12. An administrative process has a throughput time represented by the value "9T" and a queue time of "6T." What is the processing time given these parameters?

LEAN ASSESSMENT II

Section II presents the baseline assessment process and reviews the methods for examining a process from the perspectives of the product, the operator, and the machine.

Chapter 3

Lean Baseline Assessment

3.1 Baseline Definition

A Lean baseline assessment is a rigorous, team-based analysis that provides a viable alternative to value stream mapping as a way to assess the current state of a process. However, beyond this common objective, a baseline assessment embodies additional elements including consideration of a future, improved state for the process, and the development of a plan to achieve it. Specifically, the key steps for conducting a Lean baseline assessment are shown in Figure 3.1 (Fiore 2005, p. 47).

A typical Lean baseline event takes about two working days to complete. However, depending on the scope and scale of the event, assessments can last anywhere from one to five days in duration. In addition, it is highly recommended that event activities be coordinated by a Lean practitioner (an event facilitator) who is familiar with the baseline process to guide the team through the entire assessment.

3.2 Baseline Overview

Let's review each of the key steps involved in the baseline process:

- *Define the current state*: This step represents the starting point, or baseline, for initiating the overall assessment activity. A key requirement for the assessment is to recruit team members who have intimate knowledge of the process under examination. As with value stream mapping,

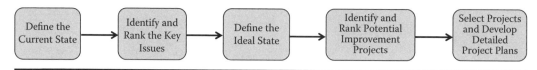

Figure 3.1 Lean baseline assessment process.

the objective for defining the current state is to gain a fundamental understanding of the existing process. This is accomplished by creating a process map (assuming that a fully defined value stream map cannot be completed), and if feasible, is supplemented with information and data that provide insight regarding the current level of process performance. In cases where process constraints inhibit the ability to create the map from firsthand observation, the process map can be created by documenting the process based on the collective knowledge and experience of the baseline participants. To ensure that the baseline event is completed in a timely fashion, the majority of effort necessary to complete the process map may be completed as pre-work ahead of conducting the actual event. The timing for this will be explained in greater detail in Section 3.4, which deals with baseline execution.

- *Identify and rank key issues*: With the current process defined, the next step is to define the key issues in the process. Once again, the expertise of the participants serves as the basis for generating and compiling a comprehensive list of problems and issues associated with the process. Depending on the number of items identified, it may be necessary to have the team rank and develop a prioritized list. The list serves as the primary resource for guiding the team on the critical areas to address.
- *Define the ideal state*: The purpose of defining the ideal state is to promote "out-of-the-box" thinking. Ideas are generated by participants by considering the design of an enhanced process with no restrictions on cost, resources, or available time. By considering the process from a "perfect-world" perspective, the ideas offered, while maybe not practical or realistic, in theory define a threshold for maximum performance. In the context of executing the entire baseline process, only a small portion of time is devoted to this activity, but it represents the foundation and inspiration for generating tangible, realistic ideas for actual implementation.
- *Identify and rank potential improvement projects*: Building on the ideas generated from the ideal state, participants generate a suite of practical improvement projects to meet a realistic, future state. Given the realities of most organizations, with limited resources available for process

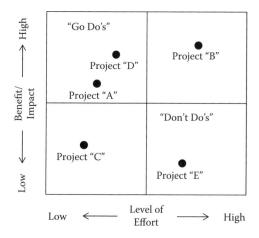

Figure 3.2 Four-quadrant model for project evaluation.

improvements, included in this step is an evaluation of the candidate projects. A simple four-quadrant model, shown in Figure 3.2, can be used for this purpose.

As you can see, the model provides a simple way to assess candidate projects in terms of the projected benefits versus the level of effort required for implementation. By superimposing projects on the map, relative comparisons can be made, leading to decisions regarding which projects to implement and establishing priorities for execution.

- *Select projects and develop detailed project plans*: With the project analysis complete, the final step is to generate detailed project plans for those projects that are deemed "above the waterline" that will proceed with actual implementation. The key elements of the project plan should include the stated objectives and goals for the project, key milestones with projected timelines for completion along with identified project team members, a team leader, and project sponsors.

3.3 Baseline Success Factors

With a fundamental understanding of the key process steps that are involved in the baseline process, we can now turn our attention to reviewing the tasks that are involved in the successful execution of a Lean baseline event. Like many things in life, the key to success in conducting a baseline event is in the preparation. The better the planning is carried out, the greater chances of success that will springboard into the project improvement and implementation phase.

There are some key components that drive event success. Let's review each of these individually:

- *Management/leadership support*: Baseline event success begins with appropriate management and leadership support. This support entails sponsorship and the designation of a management sponsor, or champion, for conducting the event. The primary duties of the champion include outlining the top-level performance goals required by the process, communicating and advocating the need for conducting the event and, as necessary, coordinating the recruitment of resources to participate and support the baseline activity. At the conclusion of the event, the champion, along with the other key stakeholders associated with the process, are the recipients of an outbrief report outlining the results of the baseline assessment.
- *Team composition*: It is critically important to have the right skill-set to support a baseline event. The majority of individuals recruited to support an event should have intimate knowledge about the workings of the process under examination. To clarify, these individuals are not mid-level managers or frontline supervisors. Rather, it is highly suggested that these baseline participants be individuals who are performing the work and are directly involved in the process on a daily basis as part of their normal job activities. To complement these people, it is also suggested to recruit one or two individuals who are not as close to the process. These people often support the process peripherally and represent internal customers who can provide a more objective perspective of the process and the issues that they encounter. Additionally, if deemed appropriate, it may be advantageous to solicit input from external, non-company individuals such as customers (recipients of the output of the process) and suppliers (providers of inputs to the process).* In terms of attendance, it is suggested that the number of participants for a baseline event range between four and nine individuals. Optimally, a range of six to seven individuals works best. From a facilitator's perspective, events with less than four people fail to provide

---

* If non-company individuals are recruited to participate in an event or provide input, careful consideration should be given to the nature of the discussions and the inadvertent disclosure of the company's proprietary information.

the richness in the discussions and the diversity desired with differing opinions and perspectives. Events with more than nine people become difficult to manage and unwieldy with too many opinions, and increase the probability of becoming bogged down on specific topics. Ultimately, this results in failure to progress through the event's agenda in a timely fashion.
- *Development of a baseline charter*: Simply stated, a baseline charter is a document that outlines the team members, scope, and objectives that are required for supporting an event (George 2002). The development of the baseline charter should begin in the early stages of formulating and planning a baseline assessment. The charter document itself serves two key purposes. First, it provides everyone who is involved with the baseline effort a clear understanding of the focus and direction for the event. Second, it serves as an excellent vehicle for communicating and educating others in the organization about the assessment activity.

The charter document is composed of different sections. Let's review each one individually:

- *Problem statement*: Provides a background on the problem at hand and answers the question of why the baseline event is being conducted. This may include information defining the magnitude of the problem and consequences to be encountered due to the lack of any established go-forward improvement.
- *Scope (in scope/out of scope)*: Identifies the starting and ending points for the process to be evaluated. It may include departments and work tasks that are to be included or excluded as part of the assessment.
- *Goals/objectives*: Defines the desired end state or level of process performance after the improvement projects (identified from the baseline event) have been implemented. Management input for this section is vital to ensure that the improvement efforts launched from the baseline activity align to the overall company objectives. Goals should always be quantified. Goal statements such as *improve the XYZ process* do not define an acceptable level of performance. Consequently, from statements such as this, it is impossible to determine if the improvement activity actually made a difference and improved the process. To avoid this pitfall, one approach is to create SMART goals. A SMART goal stands, and includes characteristics, for being specific, measurable, achievable, relevant, and time bound.

- *Deliverables*: Define the outputs. For a baseline event, the outputs are typically outlines of the identified projects to be executed to meet the desired goal. Many times, this is supplemented with a process map defining a desired future or end state condition.
- *Schedule/milestones*: Outline the schedule for go-forward planning activities, along with the completion of any identified pre-work, leading up to the execution of the actual baseline event. For example, planning preparations can include any training needed for baseline participants, confirmation of selected team members, finalization of travel plans, and other logistics. Pre-work typically includes the completion of process mapping to be completed prior to the event, along with any data collection that defines current process performance. Additional scheduling activities detailed here may include, if already determined, the reporting cadence for the improvement phase. However, in most instances, this is outlined after the improvement projects themselves have been identified.
- *Team members/sponsor*: Provides a listing of identified team members and team leader (if one has been identified), along with the event facilitator, participating in the event. The event sponsor/champion is also denoted.

Completion of a baseline charter is a key activity and establishes a solid foundation for event success. The charter can be thought of as a contract. The event sponsor, stakeholders, and participants all need to be in agreement regarding the documented information on the charter. To achieve consensus, discussions need to take place among all involved parties. The charter is merely the documented evidence of the agreed-upon decisions resulting from these discussions. In summary, a completed charter provides the following benefits:

- Demonstrates support and commitment for the event
- Establishes team direction and focus
- Promotes a teaming environment
- Provides structure and ensures an effective event planning process
- Outlines boundaries and scope
- Identifies roles

An example of a completed baseline charter is shown in Figure 3.3.

Baseline Charter

Event Title:

    Subworld store #27 Lean baseline assessment

Problem Statement:

    Sandwich preparation takes too long resulting in customer dissatisfaction and frustration. (This store takes approximately 40% longer than the company average.) During peak lunch and dinner times, customers will leave or not enter the store due to the long line.

Scope:

    All activities that take place in the Subworld store are included and considered in scope. Deliveries of materials made by suppliers are out of scope and not a part of this assessment.

Goals/Objectives:

    Produce all sandwiches, throughout the entire day, in 3 minutes (+/− 30 seconds). Achieve this level of performance within 25 days after the completed baseline assessment. Achieving this performance target would place store #27 in the top 20% of all stores.

Deliverables:

    An updated/revised process for making sandwiches and identified projects to be executed that will meet the performance target.

Schedule/Milestones:

    Day 1: Announce baseline event
    Day 21: Complete current state process map
    Day 24–25: Conduct baseline event
    Day 50: Complete implementation of improvements
    Day 51+: Monitor new process performance

Team Members/Sponsor:

Joe Smith	Mike Williams
Sally Henderson	Sue Barnes
James Wright	Larry Tate (facilitator)
Mary Jones	Janet Stevens (sponsor)

Figure 3.3 Baseline charter example.

3.4 Baseline Execution

As stated in Section 3.1, it is recommended that an individual familiar with the baseline process facilitate the team through the baseline activity. The role of the facilitator is primarily to guide the team through the process and not necessarily be a subject-matter expert with the topic or process under examination. Consequently, the primary tasks of the facilitator include guiding the team in the development of the process map(s), assisting with logistical preparations leading up to the event, facilitating the event itself by ensuring the team stays on track, and supporting discussions by offering thought-provoking and probing questions.

As a result of the experience gained from facilitating numerous baseline events, a number of considerations come into play that have proved to be instrumental for successful baseline execution. For example, the method used to bring the team members together in a working environment is an important element. Advances in net-meeting technology and electronic file sharing have afforded the opportunity for individuals to work virtually in real time, from literally anywhere across the globe. For the baseline activity, this capability has proven to be very helpful, particularly when teams have elected to complete pre-work before the actual event. However, in terms of bringing the team together for the actual baseline event, it is highly recommended that all team members be physically co-located in a room. The benefits of doing this should not be underestimated. Discussions and dialog between individuals are much more enhanced when additional context can be gleaned from face-to-face interaction. On the downside, there could be added expense to the company in terms of travel costs to bring together individuals who are geographically dispersed. But, for many companies, this cost is justified by offsetting potential inefficiencies caused by net-meeting and technical problems from virtual connections. Beyond the co-location issue, there are additional considerations regarding baseline execution related to the process itself. To review these, let's refer back to the five-step Lean baseline assessment process outlined in Figure 3.1 and examine each step individually:

1. *Step 1—define the current state*: As stated in Section 3.2, defining the current state is facilitated through the creation of a process map. To maximize the limited amount of time the team will have together during the event for discussions and collective analysis, a viable option is to complete the actual documentation of the current process as pre-work ahead of conducting the actual event. The complexity of the process will dictate

the amount of real working time needed to complete the map. As a general rule of thumb, however, it is suggested that the mapping effort be initiated three to four weeks ahead of the actual event. This allows ample time for the team not only to develop the map, but also for unforeseen issues that may arise during the course of this activity. In many instances, teams have conducted a series of meetings to develop the map, while others have successfully conducted virtual meetings to complete the task.

A variety of map formats can be utilized for documenting a process. The most basic and traditional type of process map is one that documents process activities as a linear series of connecting steps (George et al. 2005, p. 34). Following the sandwich-making theme for the baseline charter shown in Figure 3.3, an example of a basic process map is shown in Figure 3.4.

This particular example utilizes only three map symbols. The terminator symbol is used to denote the process start and end points, the rectangle to represent the process step or activity, and the diamond to indicate a decision point. Depending on the process, there are other universally accepted process map symbols that can be utilized.

Building on the basic process map, there are other map formats that can be employed. Two in particular, a swim lane map and a detailed map with noted inputs and outputs, have proven to be highly effective formats for documenting processes in support of baseline events. Each format provides its own distinct advantages. Let's review each of these in greater detail.

The swim lane map gets its name from the structure of the map itself. Each participant in the process is designated on the map and bounded by lines on either side to represent rows or columns (George et al. 2005, p. 43). This configuration creates the swim lane structure that the map is known for. The participants can be identified by whatever title is appropriate for the process: an individual (by name), job title, job function, department name, and so on. Within the body of the map, each process step/activity is superimposed and aligned in the appropriate swim lane for the participant responsible for completing that task. An example of a swim lane map (adopting the process outlined in Figure 3.4) is shown in Figure 3.5.

A key benefit of the swim lane format is the ability to easily discern hand-offs among the process participants. This is especially advantageous when there are questions regarding process flow and instances where there are perceived cycle time issues. In response to this, the process steps depicted on the map can be further supplemented with

30 ■ *Lean Execution*

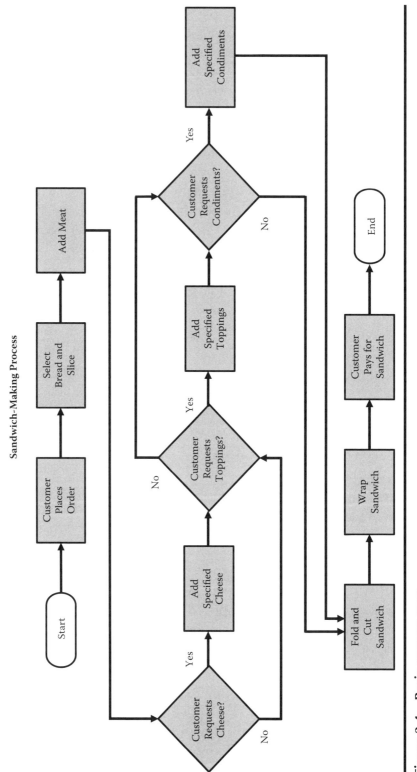

Figure 3.4 Basic process map.

Lean Baseline Assessment ■ 31

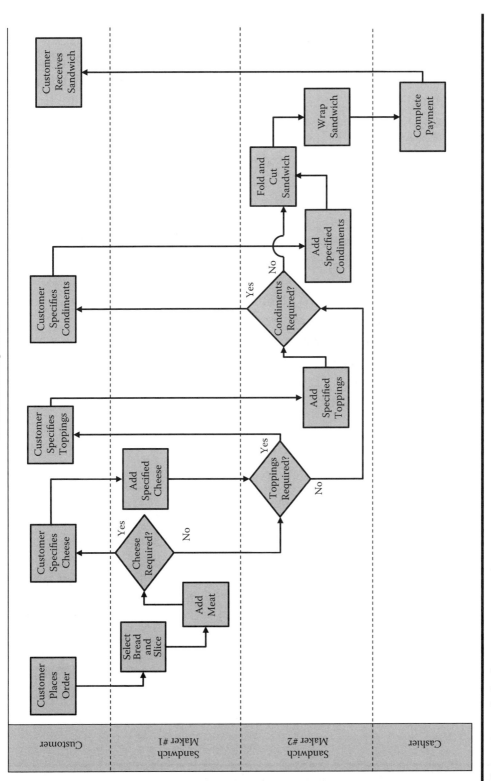

Figure 3.5 Swim lane map example.

additional information, such as inventory or cycle time data, that provides additional insight about the process.

The second map format to highlight, the detailed map with noted inputs and outputs, is essentially a modified version of the traditional process map. The structure of this map is basically the same as the traditional version, but each individual process step is augmented to include inputs and outputs related to that specific activity. Associating the inputs and outputs to each process step follows the convention shown in Figure 3.6.

As shown in the figure, the output for the process step is linked to the vertical arrow placed to the right of the process box. The inputs are listed as bulleted items directly below the process box. To realize the benefit of identifying the sources of process variation from using this format, it is first necessary to generate a comprehensive list of inputs as a precursor to identifying the root cause issues (the key process drivers) impacting the process. To identify inputs, one method that has proven to be very effective is to utilize the 6 Ms.

The 6 Ms represent elements that contribute to variation in a process. The 6 Ms, all beginning with the letter "M," are represented by the following categories:
- Man
- Machine
- Material
- Method
- Measurement
- Mother Nature (environment)

Consideration of the 6 Ms is an effective way to ensure that all aspects of the process are evaluated for possible contributors to process variation. By methodically addressing each element, items that would normally be overlooked can be captured. Using this approach, an example of a detailed process map with documented inputs and outputs is shown in Figure 3.7.

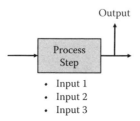

Figure 3.6 Convention for designating inputs and outputs.

Lean Baseline Assessment ■ 33

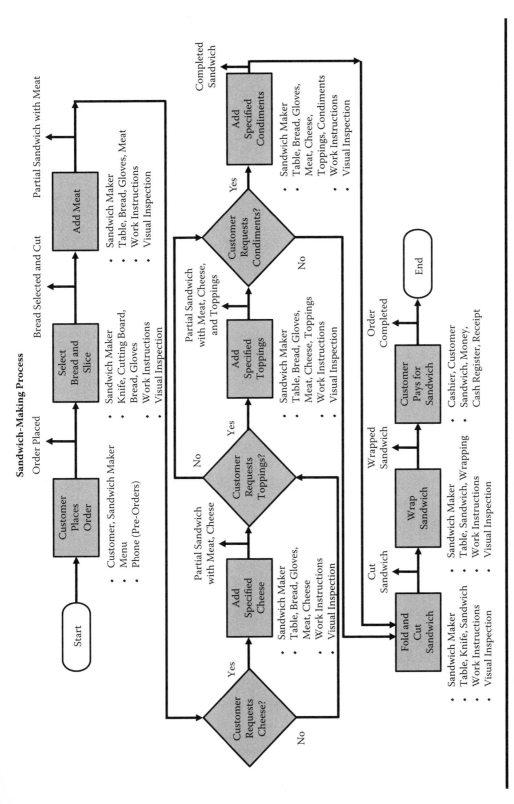

Figure 3.7 Detailed process map with inputs and outputs.

To explore the use of the 6 Ms further, let's take a closer look at an individual process step from Figure 3.7. This is illustrated in Figure 3.8.

As shown in the figure, each input has been identified and labeled with the appropriate 6 Ms element. The sandwich maker is responsible for carrying out the process activity (adding the specified cheese) and, quite obviously, falls under the *Man* category, designated for all the personnel associated with the process. Likewise, the table, bread, and so on, represent the materials needed to perform the activity, and are appropriately labeled with the *Materials* category. The work instructions outline the procedure to be followed for executing the process activity, including the standard quantity of cheese to be added to the sandwich. This information is associated with the *Method* category. Verification that the correct quantity of cheese has been added, as well as the correct placement of cheese on the sandwich, is not validated by any inspection device or machine, but rather by the sandwich maker. Consequently, visual inspection is the only measurement system, and falls into the *Measurement* category.

The review of this process step is indicative of the thought process and rationale regarding how the 6 Ms were applied to the entire sandwich-making process that is shown in Figure 3.7. There are other inputs that can be included in the map, but the underlying criteria used for identifying inputs are based on the impact to the process. For example, one could argue that the store where the sandwiches are made be included as a process input. Since the entire sandwich-making process takes place in the store, this input would be specified for every step in the process. But, if we consider this further, there is no correlation between the store and the sandwich-making process itself. In this instance, this input is essentially "a constant" and, based on its lack of impact on the process in any way, does not really warrant inclusion.

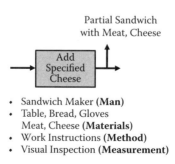

Figure 3.8   Process step with 6 Ms designations.

If, however, the process focus was related to the revenue-generating opportunities for the sandwich business, then *the store* could very well be a vital and critical input. Speculating further, root cause issues associated with the store could be related to its location, ambiance, or external appearance. In summary, all inputs, including those considered questionable regarding their impact, should be included on the map and then evaluated further to determine the real effect on the process.

2. *Step 2—identify and rank the key issues*: With a thorough review of the process map in hand, all team members can gain a fundamental understanding of the current process. In this respect, the process map is a tool and stepping stone to enable the team to proceed to the next step in the baseline assessment process—the identification of key issues impacting the process. This step is critically important to ensure that the team implements solutions to address the key drivers that influence process performance.

The identification of issues is enabled by the expertise of the individuals who are directly involved in the process. Quite simply, the people doing the work on a daily basis, and those impacted by the process, know where the problems exist. This is the reason why it is important to recruit team members who have intimate knowledge about the process. The issues are captured and documented as simple-sentence statements. Here are some examples:

- There is almost always a bread shortage during lunchtime.
- There are long customer lines during the lunch and dinner periods.
- During busy times, sandwiches are lined up in a queue in front of the cash register.
- Workers placing condiments on sandwiches are always getting in each other's way.
- Condiments are not refilled in a timely fashion.
- The cheese is shipped in large boxes and is time consuming to unpack.

With each participating member challenged to generate his or her own listing of the key issues, it is not uncommon for events to generate over 50+ issues and, in some cases, even over 100. To manage this large number, it is suggested that participants document each issue on a separate notecard or Post-it note. This is especially helpful for the next step, which is to categorize and then rank the issues based on priority.

Prioritizing the collection of identified issues is necessary because, in most instances, companies have a limited amount of resources to invest in process improvement. Consequently, it may not be possible to address all of the issues identified in a baseline event. Given the need to make choices, the prioritized list can serve as the guidepost to aid in the decision-making regarding which issues to address.

Organizing the collection of issues, as a precursor to developing a prioritized list, can be facilitated in a couple of ways. One method is to review and affinitize the entire pool of documented issues. This approach is facilitated by utilizing notecards (mentioned earlier in this section), which enable easy movement and the placement of each issue into common themes and groupings. An example of this is shown in Figure 3.9.

A second method for organizing the issues is to utilize the current state process map and have participants place each documented issue on the map in the approximate location where the problem occurs. To accomplish this, it is necessary to print a poster-sized copy of the process map to facilitate placement. An example of this is shown in Figure 3.10.

With the organization complete, the final activity is to rank the issues. There is not one absolute way to accomplish this. One option is to facilitate a group discussion in order to obtain a consensus and have the team collectively develop a ranked list. A second option is for each participant to vote independently to establish his or her own ranking, and then to consolidate the results.

3. *Step 3—define the ideal state*: As highlighted in Section 3.2, defining the ideal state is essentially a brainstorming activity to promote "out-of-the-box" thinking. The team environment established for the baseline event is a powerful catalyst to promote a thought-provoking exchange of ideas among the participants. While the ideas generated during this activity are not envisioned to be practical, the point of this exercise is to generate ideas that can be used later as a platform for establishing practical concepts for implementation.

4. *Step 4—identify and rank potential improvement projects*: Building upon the ideal state ideas, the team formulates practical solutions that represent opportunities for actual implementation. The four-quadrant model (outlined in Figure 3.2) for assessing project investment versus benefit has proven to be a simple yet, effective way, to assess and compare projects. The model also serves as an excellent vehicle for communicating to the event sponsor and management team the

Lean Baseline Assessment ■ 37

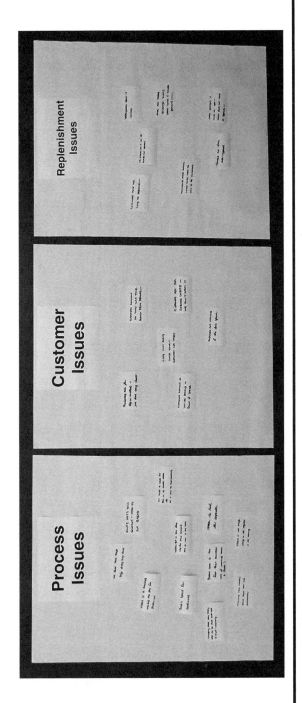

Figure 3.9 Affinitizing issues.

38 ■ *Lean Execution*

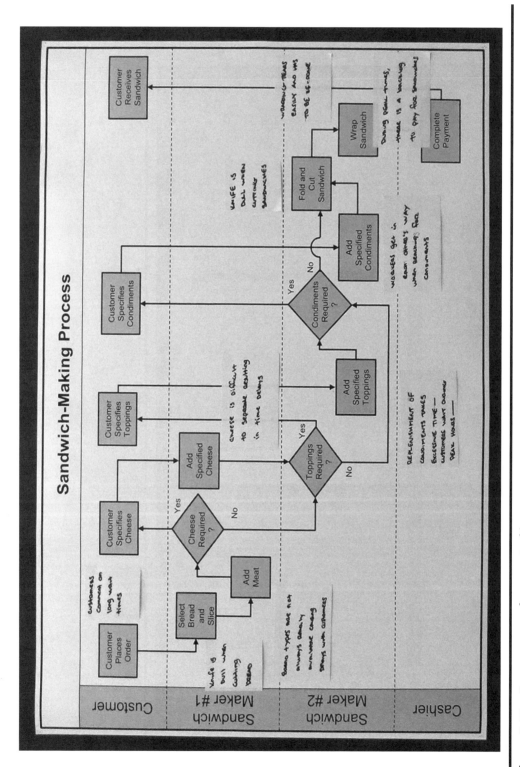

Figure 3.10 Process map placement of issues.

analysis performed to justify and recommend certain projects for implementation.

5. *Step 5—select projects and develop detailed project plans*: Projects recommended by the baseline team for implementation are further detailed with project plans. As noted in Section 3.2, it is recommended that these plans include the objectives and goals for the project, key milestones with projected timelines, and identified team members. The A3 project template has proven to be an excellent tool for outlining and documenting projects with this information.

The A3 project template is a structured problem-solving tool that documents a project on a one-page report. The name A3 is derived from the size of the paper of the template. Using this method helps to focus in on the problem, forces one to be concise in making the reports easy to read and easy to follow, and provides an ideal format to track and report results to management. Figure 3.11 illustrates a project example using the A3 template. A blank version of the A3 template is provided in Appendix B.

In terms of conducting the baseline event, time constraints may prevent the ability to fully define the project(s) with the objectives, milestones, etc. In instances when this occurs, it is highly advisable that, as a minimum during the baseline event, a leader be assigned to each project to assume ownership. By doing this, the identified individual can assume responsibility for completing the balance of the A3 template for the project after the baseline event.

Successful execution of the baseline approach is the best assurance that the right projects are selected to attack the most pressing issues. As a capstone activity to the baseline event, it is suggested that the baseline team conduct an assessment debriefing with the event sponsor and other interested parties. Performing a debriefing "closes the loop" and provides direct feedback to the attendees regarding the team's analysis and recommendations.

As noted in Section 3.1, a typical event is structured as a two-day activity. An example agenda supporting this timeline, and incorporating the elements discussed in this section dealing with baseline execution, is shown in Figure 3.12.

Also, as noted in Section 3.1, baseline assessments can certainly take longer than two days. The complexity of the process under review is typically the driving factor in judging the need for longer events. In cases where this has been determined, the basic agenda structure outlined in Figure 3.12 is still viable, but the time duration of the individual steps is greater.

Subworld Sandwich-Making Process Improvement

Date: July 30, 2015

Problem/Background

Lost revenue due to long lines during peak times. Customers leave or will not enter store upon observing long lines.

Current State

Average time at store #27 to make a sandwich is 4:10 minutes. This time is approximately 40% higher than other Subworld stores.

Lost revenue is estimated to be 15% of total daily receipts based on the number of customer that either leave or do not enter store.

Goal

Produce all sandwiches, throughout the entire day, in 3 minutes (+/- 30 seconds).

Root Cause Analysis

Analysis identified 3 key areas for improvement:

- Transportation time/distance to bread rack
- 30% time delay and backlog at condiment station
- Sandwich cutting (dull knife) and wrapping

Future State

Achieving the target goal for sandwich-making would place store #27 in the top 20% of all stores.

Implementation Plan

Task	Who	When
Move bread rack	Joe	8/3
Redesign condiment station	Mike	8/15
New knife sharpening procedure	Mary	8/10
Employee training for wrapping	Janet	8/22

Follow-Up Actions

Perform time study after condiment station redesign to verify time improvement. (Sally)

Verify wrapping procedure is performed properly. (Janet)

Figure 3.11 A3 project example.

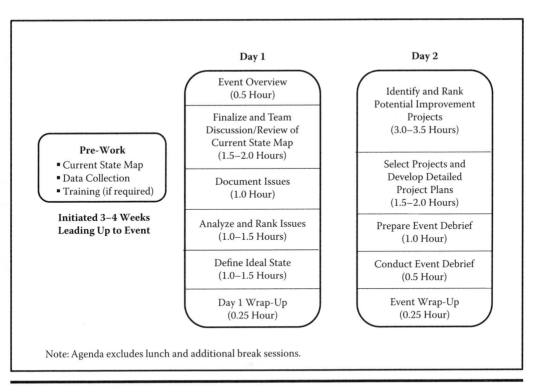

Figure 3.12 Proposed baseline agenda (two days).

To further support the execution of a baseline event, Appendix B includes worksheets for the baseline charter and a planning checklist to aid in event preparations.

A key aspect of the Lean methodology is to assess a process and identify root cause issues to improve performance. So far, we've reviewed value stream mapping and the Lean baseline assessment as methods to assess a process and identify opportunities for improvement. Fortunately, the Lean methodology employs a number of additional tools that we can utilize, in conjunction with these methods, to further assess a process and dive deeper into the fundamental issues that drive process performance.

The ability to view a process from different perspectives is the key to performing this deeper analysis. In other words, we can gain additional insight about a process if we can view it from different points of view. The following chapters in this book outline a review of a process from three different perspectives: (1) the product going through the process, (2) the operators involved in executing the process, and (3) the machines and equipment used in fabricating the product.

QUESTIONS

1. What is a Lean baseline assessment?
2. What is the purpose of the ideal state activity as part of a Lean baseline event?
3. What are the three key success factors for conducting a baseline event?
4. What role does a management sponsor play in supporting a baseline event?
5. What are the two key objectives for creating a baseline charter?
6. What is a SMART goal?
7. What is a key benefit of a swim lane–style process map?
8. What is the purpose of using a process map format that designates inputs and outputs?
9. What are the 6 Ms?
10. What is an A3 template used for?

Chapter 4

Product Analysis

4.1 Product Analysis Overview

The purpose of this analysis is to understand what is happening to the product during its journey through the process. By understanding all of the actions and activities the product is subjected to, we can assess which ones add value (value-added activities) and which ones represent opportunities for elimination or reduction (non-value-added activities).

Similar to value stream mapping, the first step in this analysis is to determine the starting and ending points for the product review. Likewise, the analysis is conducted through firsthand observation of the product as it goes through each step in the process.* Careful documentation of these observations is instrumental in assessing the specific activities and opportunities for improvement. Remember, we now have three criteria at our disposal to aid in discriminating value-added from non-value-added activities.

The documentation and assessment of the observed activities can be facilitated with a simple product analysis worksheet, an example of which is shown in Figure 4.1.

As seen in the figure, the worksheet provides a methodical way to categorize the time associated with a process. Value-added time is denoted, and non-value-added time is grouped based on the type of waste. Notes are also provided that highlight opportunities for improvement or changes that will

---

* It is highly advisable to inform all workers, as well as to seek approval from appropriate department supervisors, as to the reason for observing workers performing their tasks. Informing workers will hopefully aid in dispelling any apprehension on their part, thereby enabling them to carry out their activities in a manner that they typically perform on a daily basis.

PRODUCT ANALYSIS WORKSHEET

Part Name: **Subworld Club Sandwich** Date: **July 27, 2015** Time Units: **Sec**
Part Number: **1E389-1** Prepared By: **S. Barnes** Distance Units: **Feet**

Process Step Description	Value-Added Time	Processing Time	Transportation Time	Transportation Distance	Non-Value-Added Time — Raw Material	Storage/Queue Time — Between Process	Storage/Queue Time — End of Process	Finished Goods	Inspection Time	Notes
Receive Order	10									Order is Transformed into the Product
Select Bread	17	11								Move Bread Rack to Reduce Time
Cut Bread	17									
Add Meat	22									Re-Package Meat
Move to Counter			5	4						
Add Cheese	20									
Move to Counter			5	4						
Add Condiments	32									
Fold Sandwich		15								
Wrap Sandwich		24								
Move to Counter			6	6						
In Queue to Pay							20			
Pay for Sandwich		30								
Hand to Customer		4								
Total Time	**101**	**84**	**16**	**14**			**20**			

Figure 4.1 Product analysis worksheet.

be made to the process. A blank version of the product analysis worksheet displayed in Figure 4.1 is available for use and provided in Appendix B.

The worksheet provides a disciplined way to understand and document the activities that take place with the product as it progresses through the process. As opposed to filling out the form in real time while "walking the process," an option may be to video-record the process steps and fill out the worksheet at a later time. This also provides the added benefit of having a permanent record for future analysis and reference.

The information captured in the product analysis worksheet can also be summarized and communicated through two other Lean tools: (1) a time-value chart and (2) a spaghetti diagram.

4.2 Time-Value Chart

A time-value chart is a graphical tool to represent value-added and non-value-added activities within a process. With the data captured from the product analysis, a time-value chart not only highlights the time spent performing actual activities on the product, but also quantifies this time in comparison to the total time the product is in the process. Figure 4.2 is an example of a time-value chart (George et al. 2005, p. 52).

Referring to the figure, the horizontal line represents the timeline for the process. This can be designated in whatever unit (hours, days, weeks, etc.) that is appropriate for the process. This line is also used to distinguish the value-added activities (above the line) from the non-value-added activities (below the line). Each vertical line, on either side of the horizontal timeline, represents a specific activity being performed in the process. The thickness of each vertical line corresponds to the relative time required to complete

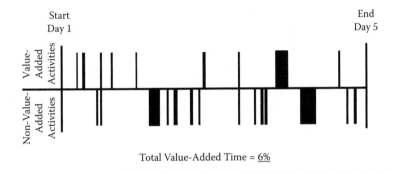

Figure 4.2   Time-value chart.

the task. The space between the vertical lines represents the queue time, or wait time, in the process.*

The percentage of value-added time is derived by dividing the total value-added time by the total process time. For example, let's say that the timeline for a process is 500 minutes and the total value-added time is 30 minutes. Therefore, the total value-added time is calculated as:

Total value-added time = (30 minutes)/(500 minutes) = 0.06 or 6%.

This is referenced on the bottom of the time-value chart depicted in Figure 4.2.

4.3 Spaghetti Diagram

A spaghetti diagram is another graphic-based tool that is used to depict the travel paths of a product through a factory. The term *spaghetti diagram* was coined because, for many companies, the travel path lines for a product depicted on the map are jumbled and random, resembling a plate of spaghetti noodles.

For a typical spaghetti diagram, the travel paths are depicted as single lines superimposed on a diagram representing the layout of the factory. The lines are connected to emulate the process sequence of the product going through the factory (George et al. 2005, p. 42).

Spaghetti diagrams can be supplemented with an additional piece of information. Work-in-process inventory, often located at various places within a factory, can be added to the diagram where it is located. The quantity of pieces of product, representing the inventory, is referenced on the map by the number in the triangle.

It is important to recognize that the inventory number represents a snapshot in time. In other words, if the spaghetti diagram was created on another day, the inventory number could obviously be different. The point of documenting inventory in this way is to recognize and understand trends. If large quantities are noted next to a particular machine, for example, it may be an indicator of a bottleneck in the process. An example of a spaghetti diagram is depicted in Figure 4.3.

---

* Lean practitioners will sometimes refer to the "white space" in a process. Specifically, in these cases, they are referring to the queue time as referenced on a time-value chart.

Product Analysis ■ 47

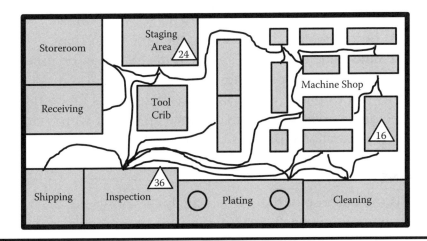

Figure 4.3 Spaghetti diagram.

The reason, for many companies, that the lines are jumbled and crisscross on a spaghetti diagram is because the factory has been laid out to align with a functional model. In this model, company resources and equipment are organized and arranged by departments and functions—machining in one area of the factory, inspection in a different location, plating and processing in another, and so on. During the course of manufacturing, if a product required multiple inspections, for example, it obviously would need to be routed to the inspection area multiple times during the course of manufacture. Multiplying this scenario for the entire process, it is not unreasonable to understand why a functional model layout often results in spaghetti diagrams depicting chaotic travel patterns.

Travel, or transportation, as we learned earlier in Section 1.6, is an example of a non-value-added activity. In Chapter 9, in our review of cell design, we'll review how the establishment of cells can minimize the impact of transportation in the factory.

4.4 Communicating with Tools

Time-value charts and spaghetti diagrams are excellent tools for highlighting the impact of non-value-added activities in a process. Due to the graphical nature of these tools, they are also excellent communication vehicles, particularly in communicating with company management teams. For example, let's say that you are making a presentation regarding your findings from a just-completed product analysis investigation. In describing the percentage of value-added time in the process, you could do so with numbers, words, and bullet points, or instead use a graphic like the time-value chart.

Tools like time-value charts and spaghetti diagrams can be used effectively to communicate not only issues and findings, but also results and improvements. For example, displaying time-value charts for both before and after a project improvement could make quite an impact with your audience and effectively illustrate the benefits from your efforts!

QUESTIONS

1. What is the purpose of the product analysis worksheet?
2. Why is one of the benefits of video-recording a product analysis?
3. What is the purpose of a time-value chart?
4. What is the meaning of different activity line thicknesses on a time-value chart?
5. What is a spaghetti diagram?
6. What is meant by the reference to *white space*?
7. The throughput time for a process is 300 minutes and the value-added time is 75 minutes. What percentage of time in this process is value-added?
8. How can a time-value chart and a spaghetti diagram be used to aid in communicating product issues?

Chapter 5

Operator Analysis

5.1 Operator Analysis Overview

From an operator's point of view, the goal from a Lean perspective is to maximize the value-added actions that workers perform in a process, and eliminate or minimize the wasteful actions. In order to accomplish this, we must first understand the actions and activities that workers perform in the process. Similar to a product analysis, the way to accomplish this is through firsthand observation and documentation of operator activities. Continuing the theme of the sandwich-making process from Figure 4.1, an example of an operator analysis is shown in Figure 5.1.

The worksheet is organized into three distinct areas to document operator tasks, categorize time, and assess opportunities for improvement. Totals can be summed for each category to demonstrate the overall impact and benefit of proposed improvements. For the example depicted in Figure 5.1, the worksheet shows that the baseline time of 99 seconds will be reduced, once the proposed changes are implemented, to 83 seconds, resulting in a 16% improvement. Once again, a blank version of the operator analysis worksheet is provided in Appendix B.

To maximize efficiency, we need to consider not only the activities that are performed by operators, but also the total quantity of work that is performed by operators. If you recall, the definition of *Lean* means to produce what is needed and when it is needed. From the company's perspective, this means that the company should not have its workers manufacture and create more products than it can sell. (This would exemplify waste in the form of overproduction—the "O" in DOTWIMP.) The ability to control the rate

50 ■ Lean Execution

OPERATOR ANALYSIS WORKSHEET

Part Name: **Subworld Club Sandwich**　　Date: **July 27, 2015**　　Time Units: **Sec**
Part Number: **1E389-1**　　Department/Functional Area: **Store #27**
Operator: **J. Smith (Process Operator #1)**　　Prepared By: **S. Barnes**

			ANALYSIS OF TIME						ASSESSMENT OF TIME		
OPERATION											
Step No.	Task Description	Time Duration	Value-Added	Tool-Related	Manual Operation	Material Handling	Walking	Change-Over	Other	Eliminate	Improve/Reduce	Leave As Is	Notes
1	Receive Order	10	10									10	Order is Transformed into the Product
2	Go To Bread Rack	4					4				2		Move Bread Rack
3	Select Bread	3				3						3	
4	Go To 1st Counter	4					4				2		Move Bread Rack
5	Select Knife	3		3								3	
6	Cut Bread	17	17								12		Change Knife Type
7	Store Knife	3		3								3	
8	Add Meat	22	22								15		Re-Package Meat
9	Go To 2nd Counter	5					5					5	
10	Add Cheese	20	20									20	
11	Return to Order Station	8					8					8	
	Total Time	99	69	6		3	21				31	52	

Value-Added = Activities that physically alter the product
Tool-Related = Activities associated with acquiring and using tools
Manual Operation = Processing activities that are not value-added
Material Handling = Activities associated with moving and packaging the product
Walking = Operator movements to acquire parts, tools, etc.
Change-Over = Workstation setup and change-over for different products

Figure 5.1 Operator analysis worksheet.

of production, and ensure that the correct quantity of product is produced within the appropriate time period, is facilitated through takt time.

5.2 Takt Time

Takt is a German term referring to the baton that an orchestra conductor uses to regulate the tempo of the music. In a Lean environment, takt time refers to the "drumbeat" or "heartbeat" of the production process. Specifically, takt time is the rate at which finished products need to be completed in order to meet customer demand.

Takt time can be expressed mathematically as:

Takt Time = Available Production Time/Customer Demand

Available production time refers to actual working hours minus time that is spent for lunch breaks, work breaks, or meetings. Customer demand refers to the number of units the customer will buy within a given time period. (Note: the time period should be consistent between the two variables in the takt time equation, whether it be per day, per shift, per week, etc.) (Wilson 2010, p. 416)

For example, a factory operates 400 minutes per day. The customer demand is 200 widgets per day. The takt time, then, is:

(400 minutes/day)/(200 widgets/day) = 2 minutes/widget

This means that for every 2 minutes, a finished product exits the process.

The takt time value has an important influence on other aspects of the manufacturing process, particularly in determining the number of operators needed for a process. By first determining the total work time (labor) required for all operators across the entire process, we can then use this information, along with takt time, to calculate the number of operators required for the process. This value, the staffing requirement, can be expressed mathematically as:

Staffing Requirement = Total Operator Work Time (labor)/Takt Time

For example, let's assume the total operator time for manufacturing product X requires 9 minutes per unit. Let's also assume the takt time for the process supporting product X is 2 minutes per unit. Therefore, the staffing requirement for manufacturing product X is:

$$(9 \text{ minutes/unit})/(2 \text{ minutes/unit}) = 4.5 \text{ operators}$$

Obviously, we cannot have half of an operator, so the rule of thumb is to round up. Therefore, for this process, we would need five operators.

5.3 Line Balancing: The Problem

The calculation in the scenario we just performed required a total of 9 minutes of operator work time, and we determined that five operators were needed to satisfy the specified takt time. A factor we have not yet considered is the distribution of the work content across the five operators, and what effect this would have on the ability to meet the takt time requirement.

We can use a Lean tool, known as a load chart, to explore this issue. A load chart is a simple bar chart displaying the work content by operator. Returning to our scenario, let's assume that the total operator work time (9 minutes/unit) is distributed across the five operators as illustrated in the load chart shown in Figure 5.2. (Note: work time has been converted from minutes to seconds.)

To further illustrate this, imagine if the operators are working side by side in an assembly line–type arrangement, with the product, after the completion of each step, being passed down the line from Operator 1, to Operator 2, and so on.

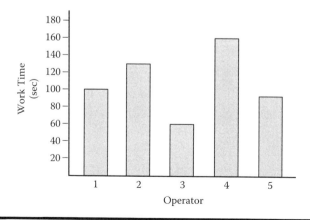

Figure 5.2 Load chart—unbalanced line.

So what effect does this work time distribution have on the process? The unbalanced distribution of the work content among the operators makes it impossible for the product to flow* and, ultimately, precludes any opportunity to meet the takt time. Operator 4's work content (160 seconds) is not only the largest, but also more than double the work content of Operator 3 (60 seconds). Consequently, as products are passed through the process, Operator 4 will not be able to keep up with the pace of Operator 3. Products will pile up in front of Operator 4, causing a bottleneck.

5.4 Bottlenecks

Simply stated, a bottleneck is a condition where the input level entering a process activity exceeds the output level. The lack of processing capacity causes a buildup of input, ultimately resulting in stagnation of the product in the value stream.

We all encounter bottlenecks in everyday life, such as rush-hour traffic and checkout lines at the supermarket. The impact of a bottleneck on a process is significant. The output of the entire system, the process, is dictated by the output of the bottleneck. In addition, process steps downstream from the bottleneck are often underutilized, resulting in increased cost and inefficiency. These conditions exemplify the management philosophy known as the theory of constraints, popularized by Eliyahu Goldratt in his book, *The Goal: A Process of Ongoing Improvement* (1992).

The theory of constraints contends that the overall output of any process is dictated by the least productive step in the process (the constraint). Consequently, to increase output for the system (the entire process), the improvement must be made at the constraint. Improvement at any other point in the process would be futile and would not be beneficial until the constraint is removed.

5.5 Garden Hose Analogy

To further illustrate the concepts regarding the theory of constraints, consider the analogy of a garden hose:

---

* Recall the definition of *flow*—the continuous movement of the product through the value stream.

Let's imagine you are watering with a 50-foot long (approximately 15-meter) garden hose. You unwind the hose and turn on the faucet. The water is flowing through the hose at the desired rate when, suddenly, the water flow coming out of the nozzle turns to a trickle. You look back along the hose line and notice, as a result of moving the hose around, that there is a kink in the line. This scenario exemplifies a very common, everyday occurrence. But, let's examine this with consideration to the theory of constraints.

In our scenario, the kink in the hose is a constraint, and it inhibits the flow of water passing through the hose. The degree of the kink has a direct impact on the volume of water coming out of the nozzle. A tight kink would allow only a small amount of water to pass, whereas a loose kink would allow a larger volume of water to pass. However, there is no correlation between the degree of the kink and the location of the kink in the hose. To clarify, it does not matter where in the line the kink is located (near the nozzle, the faucet, or somewhere in between); the output of water coming out of the nozzle is the same.

Let's say, for example, that there were multiple kinks in the line. The output, in this case, would be dictated by the tightest kink—the true constraint. The other kinks have no influence on the flow of water coming out of the hose.

What if there was a kink in the line, but you never saw it? In other words, what if the water flow was reduced, but you did not see a kink in the line and was unsure of the cause of the reduced flow? For many people, the natural reaction is to open up the faucet (assuming it was not already opened completely) to increase the input. The line of thinking here is, by increasing the input, we can compensate for the problem and increase the output. This action, obviously, does not remedy the problem. It merely builds up pressure in the line in front of the kink. Likewise, for a process in a business environment, attempting to increase input to remedy the flow problem will have the same negative result. Not only will introducing more work into the process require additional resources to manage, but also drive added complexity in the form of oversight and tracking of the increased work volume.

We can draw a number of correlations between the garden hose scenario and a company's process using the theory of constraints. Imagine the length of the garden hose corresponds to the number of steps in a process, and the diameter of the hose aligns to the workload capacity of a process. A constraint in a business process, just like a kink in a garden hose, is an impediment to flow. A large constraint, just like a very tight kink, impedes flow to a greater extent than a small constraint.

The location of the constraint in a process has no relevance on the overall process output. Whether the constraint is located in the first process step in the process, the last step, or at some point in between, the output is the same. To increase the output for the entire process, the correct approach is to identify, and then eliminate, the true constraint.

5.6 Line Balancing: The Solution

With a fundamental understanding of the issues related to flow in place, we can now turn our attention to the remedy for this situation. Referring to our earlier scenario for the unbalanced line in Section 5.3, we noted that the total operator work time (labor) was 9 minutes. To overcome the issues of the unbalanced line and eliminate potential bottlenecks, the remedy is to evenly distribute the work content among all of the operators in the process.

For total operator work time (labor) of 9 minutes, and five operators in the process, the average time per operator is 108 seconds (9 minutes = 540 seconds/5 operators = 108 seconds/operator). This means that to evenly redistribute the work content across the entire process, the target is for each operator to perform 108 seconds of work. A re-balanced line could look like the example shown in Figure 5.3.

Notice there is a slight variation in operator work content. In reality, it is probably unrealistic to have a perfectly balanced line across all operators, but the goal should be to come as close as possible. Notice, too, that the takt time value (recall from the scenario that the takt time is 2 minutes = 120 seconds) is superimposed on this load chart. Not only is the line balanced, but

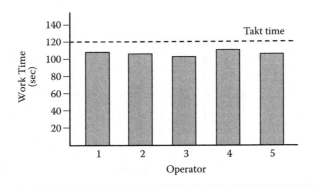

Figure 5.3 Load chart—balanced line.

the work content for each operator is below the takt time value. Satisfying these conditions is the key to achieving flow!

Recall that the takt time represents the rate of production. In Section 5.2, it was stated that the takt time value aligns to the tempo of finished products exiting the process. But what can also be stated now, as demonstrated by Figure 5.3, is that the product can flow, and be passed from operator to operator in a choreographed manner, as long as the operator work content is balanced.

In theory, matching operator work content exactly to takt time will enable flow, but in reality, this is not a very practical approach. The reason for this is the human factor (unanticipated work stoppages, worker interruptions, etc.). The general rule of thumb is to target work content to be equal to 80%–85% utilization of the takt time value. (This is illustrated in Figure 5.3 by the gap shown between the top of each operator bar and the takt time line.) This provides an adequate buffer to compensate for the human factor.

5.7 Operator Process Variation

We just learned that balancing operator content is the key to achieving flow. In our scenario, operator content was balanced around a target value of 108 seconds. Returning to the load chart in Figure 5.3, the actual work content for each operator is now added and displayed on the chart, as shown in Figure 5.4.

The numbers in the chart indicate a fairly well-balanced line. The work content values for each operator imply that for every product, the duration of work, expressed in time, should meet the specified value. The time, representing the

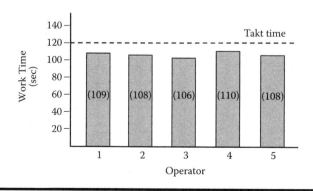

Figure 5.4 Load chart—balanced line with values.

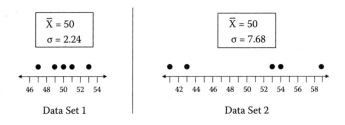

Figure 5.5 Data sets for the mean and standard deviation.

processing time for each operator, is referred to as the cycle time. (Recall this was first noted in Chapter 2 in the review of value streams.)

The cycle time values for each operator represent a target, but an appropriate question to query is the ability of each operator to consistently meet their respective target value. Operators are human beings, and once again we have to contend with the human factor. Beyond the issues previously stated in Section 5.6, other human factors that come into play include operator skills—both physical (coordination, dexterity, strength, etc.) and mental (ability to learn, technical knowledge, etc.)—experience, adaptability, fatigue level, and others. Collectively, all of these factors can have an effect, and some may change, literally, on a daily basis.

Fortunately, we can employ a Lean tool, known as a multi-cycle analysis, to assess operator variability. A multi-cycle analysis is essentially an operator time study. Multiple cycles of an operator performing a work task are timed with the data captured and cataloged on a worksheet. With measurements collected, calculations are performed to derive the average (X-bar), or mean value of the data set, and the standard deviation (σ).* The number of cycles (measurements) to run for a multi-cycle analysis can vary, and discretion should be used to determine an appropriate number to run to establish confidence in the data set.

The calculation of the mean establishes the baseline of operator performance, while the standard deviation value infers the variability about the mean. For example, consider the measurements for two data sets, each with five data points, shown in Figure 5.5.

As you can see, the mean value is the same for both data sets. However, the variation (the spread of the actual data points) about the mean is greater in data set 2, and this is reflected in the higher value for the standard deviation.

---

* Standard deviation is represented by the Greek letter sigma (σ) when referring to the entire data set population, and the "s" symbol (s) when referring to a sample of the data set.

The calculations for the mean and standard deviation are complementary and, together, provide a clear picture of operator variation. The calculation for the mean is an important measurement that represents the target, or baseline value. But this number, by itself, is one-dimensional since it does not provide any inference regarding variation. Likewise, the standard deviation calculation denotes the variation, but needs to be specified in relation to a target value, or reference point, to have proper context.

A multi-cycle analysis is an excellent tool to assess operator variability. This analysis may be performed for determining the variability of not only one operator, but multiple operators for a comparative assessment. (Refer to Appendix B for an example of a multi-cycle analysis form.)

The determination of how much variation is acceptable is subjective. The key aspect of the multi-cycle analysis is the ability to quantify the variation, thereby enabling an assessment to determine if it is acceptable, or if action should be taken to reduce it.

5.8 Ergonomics

As a final note, a review regarding operator activity would be remiss if it did not touch upon the subject of ergonomics. Ergonomics is the science dealing with the study of human interaction with the surrounding environment. From a Lean perspective, ergonomics improves productivity, removes barriers to quality, and enhances safe human performance by aligning products, tasks, and the work environment to people.

Ergonomic issues are not limited only to the factory. With advances in technology and the current extensive use with computer systems, ergonomic issues have also emerged in the office and in administrative-type settings. Ergonomic considerations that come into play include work activities associated with posture, force, velocity, repetition, duration, vibration, and others. Environmental considerations to address include issues with noise and lighting, for example.

Fortunately, at present, there are numerous products on the market that are specifically designed to address ergonomic issues. Additional remedies can include worker rotations and an increase in the frequency or duration of breaks. In summary, as part of any Lean implementation where people are involved, utilization of ergonomic principles is an important element and a key enabler for promoting a safe and efficient work environment.

QUESTIONS

1. What is takt time?
2. A factory operates 420 minutes per day. The daily output is 70 units per day. What is the takt time for the process?
3. For an administrative process, the takt time is 6 minutes per unit. If the department, excluding breaks, operates 450 minutes per day and works 5 days per week, what is the weekly output?
4. A manufacturing process is producing products to meet a customer demand of 250 units per month. What is the effect on takt time if the demand is reduced in half to 125 units, while the available working time remains constant?
5. What is the takt time for a process with 10 minutes of total operator work time and utilizing four operators?
6. How many operators are needed for a process with a takt time of 5 minutes and a total operator work time of 24 minutes?
7. Calculate the takt time for a process with the following conditions:
   a. Works a daily 8-hour shift.
   b. Each shift includes two planned 15-minute breaks.
   c. Each shift includes a planned 10-minute end-of-shift clean-up period.
   d. The customer demand requires the process to produce 160 units per shift.
8. What is a load chart and how is it used to establish flow?
9. What is a bottleneck?
10. What is the purpose of a multi-cycle analysis?

Chapter 6
Machine Analysis

6.1 Machine Analysis Overview

Analyzing the process from a machine perspective is quite similar to the approach already reviewed for the product and operator perspectives. In other words, we need to assess the process to understand the activities that are currently being performed by the machine, and then determine if any action is needed for improvement. To facilitate this, a blank version of a machine analysis worksheet is available in Appendix B.

6.2 Overall Equipment Effectiveness

To further aid the machine activity analysis, we can employ a metric known as the overall equipment effectiveness (OEE). The OEE is an aggregate, calculated metric based on three elements: (1) availability, (2) performance, and (3) quality (Nihon Puranto Mentenansu Kyōkai 1996, p. 30). The calculation for the OEE is:

$$OEE = Availability \times Performance \times Quality$$

The OEE can be applied a number of ways in a production process, such as for an individual piece of equipment, a cell, or even across an entire department. For the purposes of our discussion here, however, we'll focus on the applicability of the OEE metric for a machine.

The three elements of the OEE calculation broken down as follows (Sekine and Arai 1998, p. 189):

1. *Availability* refers to the machine being available for producing products when scheduled. In theory, when a machine is running, it is creating value for the customer. If it is not, it does not create value. Whether it is due to a tooling or operator issue, mechanical failure, or material availability, machine downtime imposes a significant cost to a company. By comparing scheduled machine run time to actual run time, the availability component of OEE allows for a determination of lost production due to machine downtime. The calculation for availability is:

   Availability = Operating Time/Planned Production Time

2. *Performance* is determined by the amount of waste created by running at less-than-optimal machine speed. Specifically, the performance component is determined by comparing the actual run rate for the machine against the ideal run rate. This allows for a determination of how much production was lost. The performance calculation is:

   Performance = (Total Units/Operating Time)/Ideal Run Rate

3. *Quality* refers to the waste that is associated with products that do not meet quality standards. By comparing the quantity of accepted parts to rejected parts, we can assess machine capability and repeatability. The calculation for the quality component is:

   Quality = Accepted Units/Total Units

To gain insight into using the OEE metric, let's use the following example and perform the OEE calculation with the data that are provided in Table 6.1:

Planned Production Time = Shift Length − Planned Shift Downtime (lunch and breaks)
   = 480 minutes − 60 minutes
   = 420 minutes
Operating Time = Planned Production Time − Machine Downtime
   = 420 minutes − 38 minutes
   = 382 minutes

Table 6.1 Data for OEE Calculation

Shift length	8 hours = 480 minutes
Shift break	2 @ 15 minutes = 30 minutes
Lunch break	1 @ 30 minutes
Machine downtime	38 minutes
Ideal run rate	50 units per minute
Production run	16,400 units
Rejected units	278 units

Availability = Operating Time/Planned Production Time
   = 382 minutes/420 minutes
   = 0.9095 or 90.95%
Performance = (Total Units/Operating Time)/Ideal Run Rate
   = (16,400 units/382 minutes)/50 units per minute
   = 0.8586 or 85.86%
Accepted Units = Total Units − Rejected Units
   = 16,400 units − 278 units
   = 16,122 units
Quality = Accepted Units/Total Units
   = 16,122 units/16,400 units
   = 0.9830 or 98.30%
OEE = Availability × Performance × Quality
   = 0.9095 × 0.8586 × 0.9830
   = 0.7676 or 76.76%

In this example, we calculated an OEE value of approximately 77%. If this was a real scenario, the next step would be to determine if this number was satisfactory or if action is needed for improvement. A key benefit of the OEE metric is that it provides three distinct areas that can be explored for improvement.

As a general rule of thumb, a calculated OEE value of 85% or greater is considered world class. The real power in tools that provide a metric and quantifiable result, like the OEE, is not merely in the generation of a number, but also the determination if the number is acceptable and what action, if any, is warranted for improvement.

The ability to make a real and lasting improvement is the primary motivation for companies in adopting the Lean methodology. With completed assessments that determine the baseline level of performance, action can be taken to exploit improvement opportunities. In Chapters 7 through 12, we will review a suite of Lean tools that represent methods and enablers to realize process improvement.

QUESTIONS

1. What is the OEE metric?
2. For an OEE value of 76%, a performance element of 94%, and a quality element of 87%, what is the availability element percentage (rounded to the nearest whole number)?
3. As a general rule, what OEE value is considered to be the threshold for achieving world-class status?

   Use the information in the following table to answer questions 4–8:

Shift length	8 hours = 480 minutes
Shift break/clean-up	45 minutes
Lunch break	1 @ 30 minutes
Machine down time	40 minutes
Ideal run rate	65 units per minute
Production run	12,000 units
Rejected units	312 units

4. What is the planned production time?
5. What is the operating time?
6. What is the machine availability percentage (rounded to the nearest whole number)?
7. What is the machine performance percentage (rounded to the nearest whole number)?
8. What is the OEE (rounded to the nearest whole number)?

LEAN IMPROVEMENT

Section III presents Lean methods for process improvement and offers guidelines for overall Lean execution.

Chapter 7

Five S

7.1 5S Overview

Five S (5S) is a methodology to transform and maintain a clean and safe work environment that supports Lean implementation. Five S provides some important intangible benefits, such as promoting a culture of order and efficiency in the workplace and raising employee morale. In addition, work areas that are clean and neat looking will gain credibility with customers, suppliers, and visitors to the company.

Five S is applicable in virtually any environment: in factories as well as in administrative areas. In addition, 5S concepts can be readily applied in the world of software and computer files. The term *Five S* is derived from five Japanese words (in the following list) representing the elements that drive the transformation in the workplace[*]:

1. Sort (*seiri*) means to clearly separate necessary items from the unnecessary. It requires the identification of what is needed to perform a particular operation or task and the removal of unneeded tools, equipment, files, parts, furniture, and so on from the work area.
2. Store (*seiton*) means to neatly arrange and create a place for each item for ease of use. It requires items to be organized based on the

---

[*] There is considerable written material on the subject of 5S. In comparing this material, and depending on the resource, it is not uncommon to find slight variations in the five Japanese terms representing the 5S methodology.

frequency of use. In addition, visual aids are often employed to easily identify the needed items.

3. Shine (*seiso*) means to perform daily cleaning and inspection of the equipment and work area. To execute this, it requires determining what to clean, how to clean, identifying who will carry out the cleaning, and what the acceptable level of cleanliness is. For equipment, inspections should be performed to ensure the equipment is in good working order and attempt to identify any non-conformities.

4. Standardize (*seketsu*) means to determine, share, and use the best processes and methods. From a 5S perspective, standardize means to ensure there are consistent and repeatable practices in place for executing the first 3 Ss (sort, store, and shine).

5. Sustain (*shitsuke*) means to maintain the implemented improvements to sustain an orderly environment, and to create a culture for future improvement (Rubin and Hirano 1996, pp. 11–27). This element embodies the Lean philosophy of embracing continuous improvement. From an implementation perspective, this is the most difficult "S" of the 5S methodology. This requires a robust operating system in which all team members who are associated with the work area actively participate. Five S does not work if one person is designated as the "5S champion", and everyone else operates in a traditional "business-as-usual" mode.

7.2 5S Implementation

Five S implementation is very easy. It does not require procurement of elaborate equipment or supplies and is a common-sense approach. For example, for simple, everyday activities like cleaning out a garage or closet, people follow the 5S methodology without formal awareness of it. To attack a messy garage, the first thing many people do is assess what's in the area and make a pile of items that they want to keep, and a separate pile for items they will discard. This is essentially the *Sort* phase of 5S.

Given the simple nature and common-sense approach that 5S signifies, 5S implementation represents an excellent starting point for companies for launching their Lean initiative. There are other important benefits from this approach. For example, what better way to get the attention of the employees in the organization, and overcome any skepticism that may exist on their part regarding the company's commitment to support the Lean implementation, than by organizing their personal work areas? In addition, successful implementation of 5S helps to create an environment and a mindset of continuous improvement and puts an organization on the path for additional success with Lean.

To facilitate the implementation of the 5S methodology, here are some tips for consideration:

- *Sort*
  - Review company guidelines for the proper disposal of unwanted and unsafe items.
  - Designate a safe and secure "holding area" for items to be discarded.
  - Tag those items that cannot be moved immediately (often referred to as "red tagging").
  - Consider recycling or selling items as an alternative to disposal.
- *Store*
  - Identify all needed equipment, tools, and supplies, and determine a location for every item. As a precursor to final placement, create a floor map or utilize tape to outline the placement and safety zone for equipment.
  - Utilize visual cues and color whenever possible. For example, shadow boards for tools and equipment, labels, large and colorful signboards, and tape outlines for walkways are all excellent examples that convey information to employees in the work area regarding the storage and placement of items.
- *Shine*
  - Stock the work area with the appropriate quantity of cleaning supplies for everyone.
  - Communicate cleaning roles and responsibilities. Everyone should participate and understand the cleaning requirements and guidelines.
  - Allocate regular cleaning time or designate end-of-shift time periods to perform cleaning.
- *Standardize*
  - Establish a cleaning checklist to ensure that the cleaning process is consistently followed.
  - Institute a review system to ensure the level of cleanliness is effectively maintained.*

---

* Recalling the garage example, often times a clean garage will return to a messy state without everyone committed to maintaining it.

- *Sustain*
    - Develop and publish a work area scorecard that communicates 5S success.
    - Develop and deploy a 5S training class for all the members of the organization, including new hires.
    - Offer incentives and awards for department or work areas that demonstrate 5S excellence.

To summarize, 5S is a foundational element and quite often a starting point for transforming an organization into a Lean enterprise. The ability of 5S to impact and touch virtually every worker in the organization is the key to the cultural impact that 5S provides. Successful 5S implementation represents a key enabler for setting the organization down the path for achieving additional benefits from its Lean implementation.

QUESTIONS

1. What is the purpose of the 5S methodology?
2. What are the environments in which 5S can be applied?
3. Why is standardization part of the 5S methodology?
4. What are some of the intangible benefits that 5S provides?
5. Which "S" is typically the most difficult to maintain and what is its purpose?
6. What are three key factors for ensuring success with 5S implementation?
7. When should 5S be implemented?
8. What role do visual cues play in supporting 5S implementation?

Chapter 8

Standard Work

8.1 Defining Standard Work

Standard work defines the amount of work performed by each operator in a process in order to achieve a balanced flow and a linear output rate. Ultimately, the goal is to meet the takt time requirement.

Standard work describes a consistent way to perform a specified task with the goal of repeatability and high quality. It represents the agreed-upon best way to perform a task and, in many instances, exemplifies a choreographed performance when multiple people are involved in the task.

There are many examples of standard work that we all encounter each and every day such as actors in a play, firefighters responding to a call, pit crews supporting a car during a race, airline pilots going through the preflight check, and so on.

For standard work to be successful, certain conditions must be met:

- Tasks should be fairly repetitive.
- Tasks should be capable of being performed by an average person on an average day. (Obviously, this statement is highly subjective, but the key is to ensure that unique skills and conditions are not required.)
- The importance of standard work should be recognized and owned by all the parties involved in the activity.
- Standard work has some variance, and it should be understood there are always opportunities for improvement.
- Ergonomic considerations should play a role in workstation layout, job sequence, tools, data, work instructions, and materials that are required.

Implementing standard work is a prerequisite to line balancing. Before action is taken to divide the total operator work time among the operators, steps should be taken to first eliminate and minimize non-value-added activities and then to establish standard work for the remaining work activities needed for the process.

The ability to establish standard work and line balancing can be influenced by machine run times. As we learned from our review of load charts in Chapter 5, individual operator content (i.e., the cycle time) must be equal to or below the takt time. Let's say, for example, that we have a process with three operators and a takt time of 30 seconds. Let's also say that a machine is required to support this process, and the machine run time, plus loading and unloading, is 50 seconds. The load chart for this example, for the operators and the machine, is shown in Figure 8.1.

Obviously, as shown by the load chart, there is a problem with establishing flow. The cycle time for the machine, which, in this example, can be interpreted as another operator in the process, exceeds the takt time. As we observed in our review of an unbalanced line, the effect of the high cycle time for the machine will result in a bottleneck being developed and the downstream process steps being underutilized.

To resolve this situation, we can return to the staffing requirement calculation and substitute *people* for *machines* for determining the number of machines needed for this process. Therefore, the calculation for the machine requirement can be expressed as follows:

Machine Requirement = Total Machine Run Time/Takt Time

Returning to our example, the calculation for the machine requirement is:

(50 seconds)/(30 seconds) = 1.7 machines

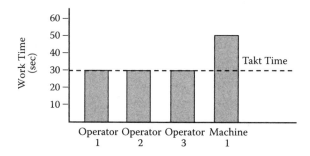

Figure 8.1 Load chart with machine.

Standard Work ■ 73

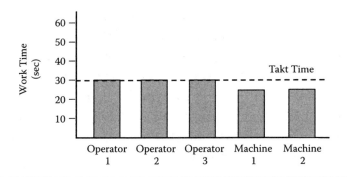

Figure 8.2 Balanced load chart with additional machine.

Similar to the staffing calculation, the number is always rounded up. Therefore, for this example, we need to increase capacity by utilizing two machines in the process instead of one in order to meet the takt time. The revised load chart, based on this calculation, is shown in Figure 8.2.

For a run time of 50 seconds with two machines, the machine cycle time is 25 seconds. This scenario, with operator and machine cycle times all equal to or below the takt time, will enable flow. For establishing the standard work for this process and ensuring flow, the cycle times for the two machines should be staggered to enable the loading and unloading of the machines to occur in a sequential fashion.

To aid in the development of standard work, we can utilize tools such as the standard work combination chart and the standard work chart.

8.2 Standard Work Tools

The standard work combination chart displays a combination of manual work time, walk time, and machine processing time for each operation in a production sequence. Using time intervals aligned to each task, the sequencing of tasks can be defined for single or multiple cycles of the process.

The standard work chart displays a graphical layout of the work area and outlines the walk paths of operators supporting the process. Major tasks of the process are summarized in a table along with associated cycle times. This chart also serves as an excellent platform for communicating the basic operation of the process.*

---

* Due to the graphical nature of the standard work chart, it serves as an excellent visual aid to display at the entrance to the work area for communicating the operation of the process.

Many versions of these charts exist and are available from a variety of sources. An example of the standard work combination chart and the standard work chart are shown in Figures 8.3 and 8.4, respectively.

These tools provide excellent vehicles for designing the overall process using standard work. After initially developed using these tools, actual trial execution of the process can commence to validate the integrity of the process design. Iterations of executing the process and refining the standard work tools may be necessary in order to develop an optimally executed process.

8.3 Adjusting Standard Work

Many industries have variable or seasonal demand. A change in customer demand, as we learned in Chapter 5, impacts takt time. (Recall that the customer demand variable is the denominator in the takt time calculation.) This, in turn, impacts the staffing requirement. (Recall that takt time is the denominator of the staffing requirement calculation.)

Consider a process with nine steps that are supported by two operators. Let's assume that the current demand is 100 units per week. If we double the demand to 200 units per week, while leaving the available time fixed, the takt time is reduced in half. Reducing the takt time in half doubles the rate of production. This means the production output needs to double given the same amount of time to complete the work.

Let's now consider the implications of this on the staffing requirement for this process. With the takt time reduced in half, and the total operator work time fixed, the number of operators needed for this process correspondingly doubles. So, instead of the original demand profile for this process requiring two operators, four operators are now required. This scenario is illustrated in Figure 8.5.

To reiterate, to support the higher demand profile of 200 units per week, the established standard work for the process would need to be reallocated among four operators instead of two. In addition to showing the process steps and work allocation for the two demand levels, Figure 8.5 also illustrates the corresponding travel paths of each operator in the process.

The ability to adjust standard work activities is an important aspect of meeting changes in customer demand. In doing so, a company can maintain efficient internal processes while demonstrating flexibility in meeting its customer needs.

Standard Work ■ 75

Standard Work Combination Chart		Plant/Facility: Food Unit #4			Date: June 17, 2015		Manual Time and Walk Time ———
		Value Stream: Sandwich			Created by: Smith		
		Product: Tuna Melt			Approved by: Jones		Machine Time - - -
		Shift: 1			Page: 1 of 1		
Step #	Process Step Description	Manual Time	Machine Time	Walk Time	Time Graph		
1	Select/Cut Bread	12		■			
2	Spread Tuna	14		3			
3	Add Cheese	8		2			
4	Toast Sandwich	6	20	3			
5	Add Toppings	15		3			
6	Package Sandwich	10		2			
	Totals	65	20	16			

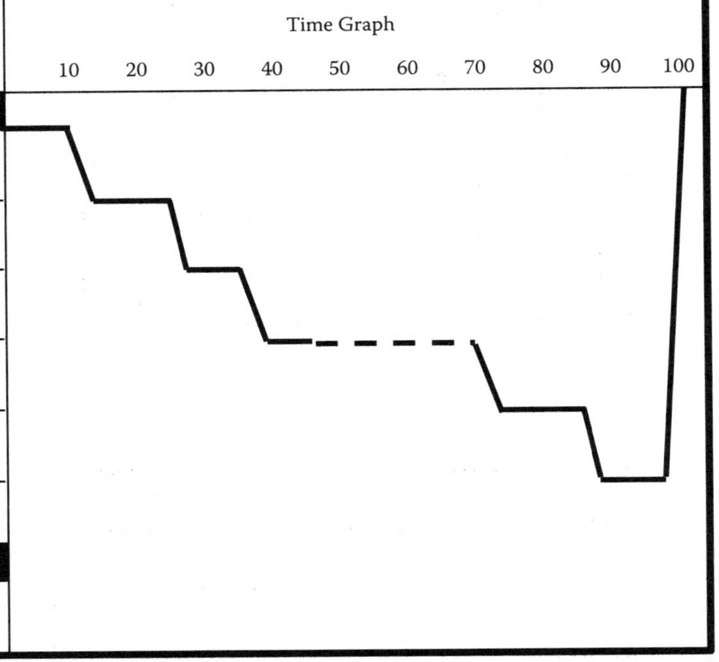

Figure 8.3 Standard work combination chart.

76 ■ Lean Execution

Standard Work Chart	Plant/Facility: Food Unit #4	Date: June 17, 2015	Production Volume: 150 Units/Shift
	Value Stream: Sandwich	Created by: Smith	
	Product: Tuna Melt	Approved by: Jones	Takt Time: 35 seconds
	Shift: 1	Page: 1 of 1	

Step #	Process Step Description	Manual Time	Machine Time	Walk Time
1	Select/Cut Bread	12		
2	Spread Tuna	14		3
3	Add Cheese	8		2
4	Toast Sandwich	6	20	3
5	Add Toppings	15		3
6	Package Sandwich	10		2
				3
Totals		65	20	16

Figure 8.4 Standard work chart.

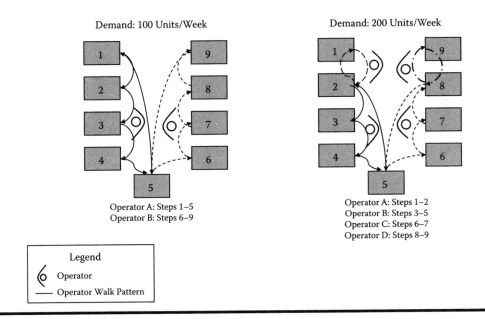

Figure 8.5 Reallocation of standard work.

QUESTIONS

1. What is the definition of standard work?
2. What are three necessary conditions to ensure success in using standard work principles?
3. Why is standard work a prerequisite to line balancing?
4. How many machines are needed for a process with total machine run time of 115 seconds and a takt time of 40 seconds?
5. What is the purpose of the standard work combination chart?
6. What tool is used to communicate the basic operation of a process?
7. Why is it necessary to adjust standard work?

Chapter 9

Cell Design

9.1 Cell Definition

A cell is a grouping of people, workstations, machines, and equipment dedicated to producing a designated group of products. In a Lean environment, the purpose of a cell is to increase flexibility for producing a high variety of products in small batch sizes while concurrently maintaining the productivity benefits attributed to large-scale production.

As opposed to the traditional production model where company resources are grouped together by function and largely dispersed in different areas of the factory, the cellular model brings together and co-locates all of the required resources in a central location.

There is no solely preferred configuration for designing a cell. There are a variety of cell designs with each one possessing different characteristics (Black and Hunter 2003, p. 210). This is summarized in Figure 9.1.

Proper cell design requires great care and planning. Considerations related to cell location include proximity to docks, material feeder and storage locations, and special processing facilities. For the cell design, the layout should consider equipment access for maintenance and repair, materials flow with the cell, and tool storage. From a worker perspective, consideration is imperative for operator safety while working in the cell; travel paths; ergonomic issues related to workstation design, access to materials, equipment, and tools; and communication among workers in the cell (Black and Hunter 2003, p. 258).

Design Type	Cell Characteristics
	• Ideal for craft work • Supports products with high takt time and typically low cycle times • Product changeover cumbersome • Low product variety
	• Easily expandable • Easy-to-follow flow • Easily accessible (from both sides) • Allows for straight-line handling methods
	• Easy expansion for high fixed assets located in turn area • Accommodates storage location (inside "L") • Supports physically long operations in limited space
	• Adjacent inflow and outflow accommodates material handlers along an aisle • Facilitates worker communication • Reduces travel and walking paths • Provides control of material located in center
	• Easy line access at multiple points • Segregated branches to accommodate different functions • Permits multiple routings with automated processes, handling, and controls • Supports flexible manufacturing with two-level conveyors or robotics

Figure 9.1 Cell design types and characteristics.

The list of items for consideration when designing a cell is extensive. But with appropriate planning, a cell can be designed that will perform efficiently and meet the company's performance objectives.

9.2 Visual Systems

Visual systems play an important role in cell design. In Chapter 7, we noted the importance of visual cues in conveying information to employees. This is critical for ensuring the successful operation of the cell. A visual system, quite simply, is a suite of devices designed to provide information at a glance (Hyer and Wemmerlöv 2002, p. 99, 164). We all encounter elements of visual systems in everyday life. For example, imagine trying to navigate on city streets without traffic signs or traffic lights?

There are basically two types of visual system devices:

1. *Visual displays*—provide data and information. Examples of displays include street signs, performance charts, and metrics postings.
2. *Visual controls*—control or guide the actions of people. Examples include parking lot lines, no-smoking signs, and traffic lights.

In the design of a cell, a visual system representing numerous devices can be employed. Examples of visual devices that can be utilized in the design of a cell include the following:

- Shadow boards for tools and equipment
- Labels and floor lines for supplies, storage, and traffic areas
- Charts displaying cell performance and productivity metrics
- Lights that are activated to alert management and support personnel of a quality or production problem requiring assistance. (These are known as andon lights.)
- Signs that highlight safety requirements, hazardous materials, or machine operation

This list can be considerably longer, but the point here is to provide examples that highlight the important role that a visual system can play to support successful cell operation.

9.3 Group Technology

In many instances, a cell is designed to support more than one product. However, a prerequisite for producing multiple products in a cell is that they can be manufactured with the equipment and resources available in the cell. This requirement implies that all the products produced in a particular cell follow a similar production process. Once again, the interpretation of "similar" in this case is very subjective. Fortunately, however, we can use a tool that is known as a product–process matrix to assess the level of commonality among a group of products. This concept of assessing the level of commonality for a collection of parts or products is known as *group technology* (Black and Hunter 2003, p. 59).

The product–process matrix is a spreadsheet-type tool organized with candidate products referenced in rows and individual process steps or equipment specified in columns. Within the body of the spreadsheet, marks are indicated for each product that requires the use of that specific process step or equipment during production. An example of a product–process matrix is shown in Figure 9.2. Note that this example references a manufacturing process. The product–process matrix can be used for virtually any type of process, including non-factory applications.

The marks provide a graphical display representing the level of commonality across the entire grouping of products. To gain additional perspective regarding the degree of commonality, the product–process matrix can be augmented to specify the sequence and cycle time for each process step. Updating the matrix from Figure 9.2, the modified matrix displaying this information is shown in Figure 9.3.

The product–process matrix is a powerful tool to aid in determining the level of commonality for a product grouping. With a completed matrix, informed decisions can be made regarding product compatibility to support the cell design.

	Machining (3-Axis Machine)	Milling	Machining (5-Axis Machine)	Turning	Grinding	Polishing
Product A	X	X	X	X	X	X
Product B	X		X		X	
Product C		X		X	X	X
Product D	X	X			X	X
Product E	X		X	X	X	
Product F		X	X	X	X	

Figure 9.2 Product–process matrix.

	Machining (3-Axis Machine)	Milling	Machining (5-Axis Machine)	Turning	Grinding	Polishing
Product A	1, 2:35	2, 1:08	3, 2:04	4, 0:45	5, 1:10	6, 0:47
Product B	1, 2:18		2, 1:50		3, 1:05	
Product C		1, 1:56		2, 1:10	3, 1:29	4, 0:35
Product D	2, 3:12	1, 1:10			3, 0:48	4, 0:32
Product E	1, 2:48		3, 1:49	2, 1:13	4, 1:02	
Product F		1, 1:29	3, 2:02	2, 1:42	4, 0:58	5, 0:56

Figure 9.3 Modified product–process matrix.

QUESTIONS

1. What is a cell?
2. What is the purpose of a cell?
3. What are some key factors to consider when selecting a cell location?
4. What are some key factors to consider when configuring the cell design?
5. Why is a visual system an important element in cell design?
6. What are the two basic types of visual devices and what is the purpose of each?
7. What is group technology?
8. What is a product–process matrix?

Chapter 10

Process Improvement Enablers: Setup Reduction, Total Productive Maintenance, and Mistake-Proofing

10.1 Setup Reduction

The concepts for setup reduction were developed by Shigeo Shingo in the 1960s. Setup reduction is commonly known by the acronym SMED, which stands for single-minute exchange of die. The philosophy was born in the automotive industry, where historically, the setup times for the dies of large press machines were extremely long. Under SMED, the goal for a setup is less than 10 minutes. (Hence, the "SM" in SMED implies *single-digit minute*.) (Shingo 1985, p. 22)

The underpinning for setup reduction opportunities is DOTWIMP.* In other words, just as we identify non-value-added activities and classify waste in terms of the seven categories represented by DOTWIMP, so too can we for setup reduction. Examples of waste activities associated with setup reduction include requisitioning tools, excessive recalibration, and waiting for the first-run piece inspection.

---

* Recall from Chapter 1 that the acronym DOTWIMP represents the seven categories of waste. The first letter of each category (defects, overproduction, transportation, waiting, inventory, motion, and processing [unnecessary steps]) is used to represent DOTWIMP.

Operationally, the way to attack setup time is similar to the approach that was reviewed in Chapters 4 through 6 for analyzing a process for identifying waste opportunities. To accomplish this, the initial step is to gain a fundamental understanding of the activities currently being performed for setup. This is facilitated through firsthand observation along with appropriate documentation of the specific tasks (see Appendix B for an example of a setup time analysis worksheet that can be used for this purpose). Armed with the three criteria that define value-added activities, opportunities for waste elimination and reduction can then be identified.

Using SMED, actions that represent setup time can be classified in one of two ways (Shingo 1985, p. 22):

1. *Internal setup time*—the machine must be stopped to perform the action.
2. *External setup time*—the action can be performed while the machine is running.

Strategically, to reduce the overall setup time, the goal is to maximize the external setup time and reduce the internal setup time. A good example that illustrates this objective is a race car pit crew. In this situation, fractions of a second can make the difference between winning and losing a race. Consequently, the crew takes advantage of every opportunity to complete the preparations while the race car is on the track. Once the race car enters pit row, crews work as quickly as possible to complete their tasks to get the car back on the track. In this case, maximizing external setup time by even the smallest amount can make a critical difference. Incidentally, this is also a good example of standard work.

Reducing setup time is a key enabler to support the production process. Smaller setup times allow for smaller batch sizes, thereby enabling production to be more responsive and more closely reflect true customer demand. Internally, smaller batch sizes free capacity, improve scheduling and flexibility, and reduce inventory and lead time.

Consider the scenarios depicted in Figure 10.1. The batch size, and the corresponding setup time, is greater for scenario 1 and graphically depicted by the larger rectangles.

Scenario 1, with only one product completed each day, takes four days to complete four different product types. Scenario 2 utilizes batch sizes that are half the size of scenario 1, with correspondingly smaller setup times.

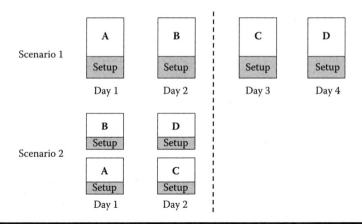

Figure 10.1 Contrasting batch sizes.

Consequently, after day 2, scenario 1 has completed only two products, while scenario 2 has completed all four products.

To summarize, reduced setup times afford the ability to produce products in small batches within a given time period. This leads to a host of operational benefits that give companies that are successful with SMED a distinct competitive advantage.

10.2 Total Productive Maintenance

Total productive maintenance (TPM) is a proactive approach to maximize the operational effectiveness of machines and equipment. TPM strives to achieve this by ensuring that machines suffer no breakdowns, are not subjected to small stops and slow running, and produce no defects, all while maintaining safe operation with no accidents.

TPM plays a critical role in supporting a Lean enterprise. With minimal inventory levels, any equipment failure can have an immediate and significant impact in meeting takt time and the production schedule. A comprehensive TPM program requires participation by all individuals who are involved with equipment use and support.* Consequently, an effective TPM program is facilitated by placing a strong emphasis on empowering operators and support personnel to help maintain the equipment.

The TPM methodology is based on seven pillars that outline proactive and preventative techniques for improving equipment reliability:

---

* The word *total* in *total productive maintenance* is included for this reason.

1. *Autonomous maintenance*—incorporates general maintenance activities carried out by the operator such as cleaning, inspection, and lubrication.
2. *Planned maintenance*—includes regularly scheduled maintenance tasks based on predicted and established failure rates.
3. *Quality maintenance*—deals with the application of root cause analysis to eliminate recurring sources of quality defects.
4. *Focused improvement*—utilizes small groups of employees working together proactively to improve machines and equipment.
5. *Early equipment management*—leverages knowledge and acquired firsthand experience gained through TPM in the design of new equipment.
6. *Training and education*—conducts training for meeting TPM goals and objectives.
7. *Health and safety environment*—maintains a healthy and safe work environment.

In line with the Lean philosophy, the overarching objective of TPM is the elimination of waste (Sekine and Arai 1998, p. 2). From the machine perspective, this waste is in the form of equipment downtime, scrap, defects, wasted energy, labor inefficiency, and accidents. As we reviewed in Chapter 6 for machine activity, the ability to measure this waste quantitatively is through the overall equipment effectiveness (OEE) calculation. An effective TPM program is the remedy to address a low OEE number.

10.3 Mistake-Proofing

People make mistakes. Mistake-proofing is a philosophy that recognizes the inevitability that mistakes will occur. The mistake-proofing approach uses common-sense ideas and methods, in both the process and the product, to eliminate human and mechanical errors.

Mistake-proofing is another technique developed by Shigeo Shingo as a tool to achieve zero defects. The premise for mistake-proofing is that by taking over repetitive tasks or actions that depend on memory or vigilance, workers are free to pursue more value-added activities (Shingo 1986, p. 99).

Mistake-proofing solutions can be applied to any process. But from a practical perspective, the focus for implementation should be on critical process steps and activities.

Mistake-proofing solutions fall into one of two categories—(1) those that prevent defects and (2) those that detect defects. From a business perspective, prevention (recognizing that a defect is about to occur) is better than detection (recognizing that a defect has occurred).*

Mistake-proofing methods and solutions can be quite varied (Shingo 1986, p. 99). These include the following:

- *Counting and grouping methods*—methods that check for correct part quantities
- *Motion-step or sequencing methods*—methods that check process steps to ensure that the sequence order is correct
- *Physical or contact methods*—methods that check physical characteristics, such as diameter or temperature

Mistake-proofing solutions are employed in many products that we all use each and every day. Tethered gas caps for automobiles, safety handles on lawn mowers, and clearance bars at entrances to parking garages are examples of mistake-proofing devices, just to name a few.

Successful implementation of mistake-proofing is a key enabler in minimizing defects. This, in turn, reduces waste, enabling the company the ability to commit more resources to value-added activities.

QUESTIONS

1. Why is setup reduction an important element to support Lean improvement?
2. What is the difference between internal and external setup time?
3. Strategically, what is the goal regarding the relationship between internal and external setup time?
4. What is TPM?
5. Why is TPM important for a Lean enterprise?
6. What is the premise for using mistake-proofing concepts?
7. Why is the prevention of a defect better than the detection of a defect?
8. What are the three basic types of mistake-proofing methods?

---

* Recognizing that a defect is about to occur is predictive, whereas recognizing that a defect has occurred is reactive. From a business perspective, preventing a defect from occurring (predicting) is preferable to finding a defect (detecting) from the standpoint of producing defective products that would need to be either scrapped or reworked.

Chapter 11

Materials Management

11.1 Materials Management Overview

The management of material through a value stream is an important element to ensure flow and maintain overall process efficiency. This issue has an impact at the very beginning of the value stream, with the customer establishing the product demand.

As we previously reviewed in Chapter 5, a company's value stream is engaged, and paced, in response to the customer demand. From the company's perspective, the goal is to have a constant level of demand, reflected by the takt time. However, a number of factors may come into play that can cause variation in the company's internal demand schedule. Examples include end-of-period sales incentives, expedited orders, or production schedule changes (customer pull-ins and push-outs).

Variable demand can cause chaos within a company's operations. Inventory levels increase to support demand changes. Likewise, this translates into increased lead times and reduced available floor space due to the need to support higher levels of work-in-process (WIP) inventory.

In response to variable demand, companies at times will attempt to influence demand patterns. Discounts offered on selected days or times of day, or specials to selected demographics of the population are examples where companies seek to increase business during low-demand periods. In other cases, companies may attempt to renegotiate delivery schedules with existing customers.

In periods of high demand, companies may increase capacity. Typically, this is done in one of two ways: (1) hiring more workers, or (2) working overtime.

Working overtime increases the available work time. Consider this with respect to the takt time calculation. For example, let's say that for an established process, a new customer order comes in that doubles the current demand. Recall that the demand variable is the denominator of the takt time calculation. In response to this, let's say that we can double the available work time by adding another shift. Recall that the available work time variable is the numerator of the takt time calculation. Therefore, by doubling the available work time in response to a doubling of the customer demand, we've maintained the same ratio, thereby maintaining the same takt time.

In addition to customer demand, material availability also has an influence on process flow. If materials are not available when needed, the value stream cannot be engaged. Likewise, if material is not available at the appropriate time during the production cycle, the operation of the value stream will stall. To avoid these situations, we can employ Kanbans to ensure material is available when needed.

11.2 Kanbans

The term *Kanban* is a Japanese word that means *signboard*. In a Lean production environment, a Kanban is used essentially as a signal. The Kanban signal itself can be virtually anything: an empty box, a fax, an electronic signal, a light, a buzzer, and even an empty space on the floor (Wilson 2010, p. 138). There are two basic types of Kanbans:

1. Material Kanban
2. Production (or in-process) Kanban

Material Kanbans are used to replenish material consumed by the production process. Material Kanbans often extend beyond factory walls to include suppliers. Kanban levels can be calculated based on a number of factors such as supplier replenishment time, the average daily consumption rate, a safety factor (a buffer stock quantity), and others. A myriad of Kanban calculations are available and can be used representing varying degrees of complexity. In reality, the Kanban calculation, although mathematically based, is really just an estimate due to the need for certain assumptions to be made

(Wilson 2010, p. 176). In some cases, equally valid, but slightly different, assumptions can change the calculated Kanban result by 30% or more.

Production, or in-process Kanbans, are signals to pace the movement of products in a process to ensure flow. Figure 11.1 demonstrates an example of a production Kanban.

In theory, if the production line was perfectly balanced and operating in accordance with the takt time, there would be no need for a production Kanban. In practice, however, production Kanbans are often used to account for the inherent variations in flow that exist in many processes. Some factors that contribute to this variation include the following:

- *Mismatched cycle times*: Within a process, some individual steps may have very short cycle times, whereas others are considerably longer. This mismatch can cause issues in achieving a balanced line.
- *Transportation distance*: Some processes, particularly those where suppliers are located far distances away, can impact flow.
- *Long lead time or process instability*: The unpredictability of excessive lead times and unforeseen process issues can also impact flow.

Utilization of a Kanban becomes effective only after a process has reached an appropriate level of maturity. This maturity implies that the quality levels of both the product and process are stable, demand variability is understood, customer and supplier relationships are established, processes are documented, and standard work is used. Along with these process conditions, effective Kanban use is facilitated through adherence to six rules.

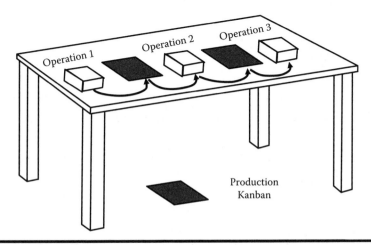

Figure 11.1 Process using production Kanban.

These rules, outlined as follows, were originally proposed by Taiichi Ohno during the development of the Toyota Production System:

1. Defects and incorrect quantities are never sent to downstream processes.
2. Customers (i.e., downstream processes) withdraw items in the specific quantities that are dictated by the Kanban.
3. Suppliers (i.e., upstream processes) produce items in the specific quantities dictated by the Kanban.
4. No items are made or moved without a Kanban.
5. A Kanban should be utilized every time and for each item.
6. Kanbans should be reduced carefully to lower inventories and uncover process issues.

In summary, a Kanban can be instrumental in supporting flow, provided that process fundamentals are in place as prerequisites to maximize its effectiveness.

11.3 Little's Law

We can further exploit the use of Kanbans by considering the variables in Little's law. Little's law (George et al. 2005, p. 202) states that the average number of customers in a system (over some interval) is equal to their average arrival rate, multiplied by their average time in the system.* Symbolically, we can use Little's law and express the relationship in a Lean system for WIP, throughput, and queue time mathematically as:

$$WIP = Throughput \times Queue\ Time$$

where
  WIP = average work in process (average number of units in the queue),
  Throughput = average number of units that are completed in a given time interval (units/time), and
  Queue time = average time that a unit stays in the queue (cycle time of the queue).

---

* In 1961, John D.C. Little published a paper in *Operations Research* providing a proof for the queuing formula.

To illustrate the use of Little's law, consider the following example:

A factory process produces an average of 300 units per day and has an average WIP level of 1200 units. What is the process queue time to complete the units that are in the queue?

Utilizing the equation and solving for the queue time, we can rewrite Little's law as follows:

$$\text{Queue Time} = \text{WIP}/\text{Throughput}$$

Therefore,

$$\text{Queue time} = (1200 \text{ units})/(300 \text{ units/day}) = 4 \text{ days}$$

Queues are an indicator of process health. Large queues are indicative of an unstable and immature process. By understanding the relationship between WIP, throughput, and queue time using Little's law, we have insight regarding the effect each variable has on the process. For example, as shown by the equation, reducing WIP will reduce the queue time. Little's law represents another tool that we can leverage for additional process improvement.

QUESTIONS

1. What effect does variable demand have on a company's production schedule?
2. In what ways can a company attempt to influence demand patterns?
3. What can a company do to increase capacity during high-demand periods?
4. What is the effect on takt time if the customer demands doubles and the available work time remains constant?
5. What are the two main purposes of Kanbans?
6. What are the three factors that contribute to the inherent variation that exists in processes?
7. What are the key prerequisites to have in place in order for the use of Kanbans to be effective?
8. A factory process has an average WIP level of 1200 units and a process queue time of five days. What is the throughput (production in terms of units per day) for this process?

Chapter 12

Knowledge Management

12.1 Knowledge Management Overview

For factory processes, where the thing going through the process is a physical product, the practice of identifying waste is a pretty straightforward proposition. Since the product can be seen and tracked, it is easy, for example, to identify non-value-added activities such as the transportation of the product from one machine to the next, or high levels of work-in-process inventory scattered across the factory floor. Quite simply, identifying waste opportunities can be accomplished by direct observation of the product in the factory.

For transactional and administrative processes, the thing going through the process is not a physical product, but rather information. Consequently, since information cannot be directly seen or tracked, the task of identifying waste is a little more challenging. For example, visual cues such as an overloaded inbox or a messy desk with scattered papers could be indicators of an overworked employee, representing a bottleneck in the process.

By considering factory and non-factory processes in this way, we can draw a correlation between the things going through the process. This is illustrated in Figure 12.1.

To gain efficiencies in administrative processes requires a focus on information. Raw data, company knowledge and intellectual property, and even employee expertise are all components of information. The ability to effectively manage these components, under the umbrella of knowledge management, is a key enabler to realize improvement not only from transactional-type processes, but also all processes.

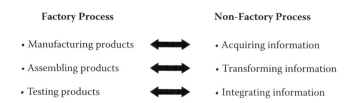

Figure 12.1 Correlation between factory and non-factory processes.

12.2 Knowledge Management System

Many people think that knowledge management is another way to refer to data repositories and file management systems. This is not the case. Knowledge management is a system consisting of processes, human behaviors, and tools that enable individuals to access the right information, at a time when it is needed, in order to make the right business decisions.

Let's explore the topic of knowledge management more closely by explaining how we define *knowledge*. Knowledge, in itself, can be represented as two different types: (1) explicit knowledge and (2) tacit knowledge.

Explicit knowledge represents data that can be communicated, documented, and stored in computer systems. It represents data possessing characteristics of being factual, discrete, and can be articulated and transferred. Examples include data found in manuals, books, procedures, videos, presentations, and pictures, to name a few.

Tacit knowledge, on the other hand, is knowledge that resides in people's minds. It is the expertise, judgment, skills, experience, tribal knowledge, awareness, and wisdom that each person possesses. Tacit knowledge is acquired through practice, is prone to subjective insights and emotion, and is inseparable from individuals (Collison and Parcel 2004, p. 18).

For example, let's assume that you want to become a great golfer. A logical approach would be to gather as much information as you can regarding the proper technique for swinging a golf club. You could read books on the topic, watch videotapes, and even attend golf clinics. In other words, the explicit knowledge to learn how to become a great golfer is readily available to virtually anyone. Would scrutinizing this material, even to the point where you could recognize a perfectly executed golf swing, make you a great golfer? The answer, obviously, is a resounding no.

Becoming a great golfer requires, for most people, many, many hours of practice. It means repeating the golf swing over and over again and making corrections as needed. It requires an understanding of the characteristics of the golf course itself: tall versus short grass, firm versus soft greens, wind conditions, and many others. This knowledge, tacit knowledge, is gained only through the firsthand experience of playing and practicing golf. In summary, it is the combination of explicit and tacit knowledge, together, that is the recipe for producing a great golfer.

Consequently, improving a company's knowledge management practices typically requires a combination of solutions. Explicit knowledge can be enhanced with improvements in processes and information systems with readily accessible data. Tacit knowledge can be addressed with training, pilot programs for new hires, and mentoring programs, among others.

The marriage of explicit and tacit knowledge is critical for ensuring that employees execute their activities as efficiently as possible. Companies that recognize the power in this combination, and foster an environment of employee learning and continuous improvement, are the ones that are truly successful.

QUESTIONS

1. Why is identifying waste typically a more difficult proposition for administrative processes than for factory processes?
2. What are the three components of information?
3. What is knowledge management?
4. What are the two types of knowledge and what are their differences?
5. How can knowledge be improved?

Chapter 13

General Guidelines for Lean Implementation

13.1 Lean Perspective

The Lean methodology has a track record of improving processes for many companies. The degree of success, however, is influenced by many factors. Companies that have been truly successful in using Lean methods understand that Lean is not an initiative that is started at some point and then stopped but that Lean represents a philosophy that touches the company's culture and defines the way to run the business. For Lean to work to its full extent, it must touch and permeate all the levels of the organization. Companies that embrace Lean understand that they will never be finished with Lean—it is a never-ending endeavor.

13.2 General Guidelines

The topics covered in this book represent core elements for successful Lean process implementation. While there is, of course, no prescribed way to implement Lean, the nature of the tools and methods infer a logical progression of usage. Based on this, the following general guidelines are offered to support your Lean process improvement:

- *Process improvement is like a journey.* It has a starting point and a destination in mind. Lean tools provide the way to gain insight about the process. This insight serves as the guideposts for navigating along the path and implementing improvements to achieve the end state.
- *In most situations, it is easy to recognize when something is not working, but, it is often not easy to identify why it is not working, what the root cause is, as well as the magnitude of the problem.* In the case of a business process that is not working, the starting point for the improvement journey is to create a value stream map. A value stream map provides a top-level view assessing the current state of the process and identifies the key issues to address.
- *For processes that are not readily accessible, and for conditions that prohibit the creation of a value stream map, an alternative is to perform a Lean baseline assessment.* This provides a viable option for assessing the current state by leveraging the expertise of employees who are involved in the process.
- *With key issues identified, the next step is to perform a deep-dive and root cause analysis.* This is accomplished by conducting a thorough interrogation of the process from the perspective of the product, the operator, and the machine. To get to the root cause requires a fundamental understanding of the actions and activities that take place, and this is accomplished from firsthand observation of the process from each perspective. Armed with criteria that define value-added activities, wasteful activities can be identified that represent opportunities for waste elimination or reduction.
- *Assessing the magnitude and degree of waste opportunities can be highlighted with the use of tools like a time-value chart and a spaghetti diagram.* An important aspect of using these tools is to be mindful of the information they convey. For example, if there is a need to understand the amount of transportation in the factory required for a product, or where work-in-process inventory is scattered about the factory floor, a completed spaghetti diagram can provide this understanding.
- *Essentially, the process improvement journey is really about asking questions and learning.* The application of Lean tools is the opportunity to answer these questions and obtain information about the process. The key in doing this, however, is to use the right tool to generate the correct information in response to the question that is being asked.
- *The culture of an organization and the willingness of employees to embrace change are key factors in the execution of a Lean-based process*

improvement. Implementing a 5S program is an excellent way to begin the transformation. Five S is an enabler that physically transforms work areas, directly impacts employees involved in the process, and lays the foundation for instituting follow-on process changes.

- *The development of a streamlined process strives to maximize value-added activity and eliminate or minimize waste.* Waste elimination and reduction are precursors to any attempt to establish flow in a process. This is necessary because, obviously, it does not make sense to establish flow for activities that should not even be in the process.
- *Once all waste has been eliminated or reduced, the process can be standardized with the establishment of standard work.* The ability to assess variation in operator activities through a multi-cycle analysis is a key enabler to facilitate the creation of standard work. With a standard process defined and an understanding of the infrastructure (equipment, tools, and other facilities) needed to support production of the product(s), consideration can then be initiated for designing a cell.
- *Cell design begins with an establishment of takt time.* This value, plus the total operator time derived from the standardized process, can be used to determine the staffing requirement. Work content can then be divided to create a balanced line using a load chart. If appropriate, the product–process matrix can be used to evaluate other candidate products to represent a family of products to be supported by the cell.
- *The actual location and layout of the cell should take into account numerous factors.* Logistical issues, operator safety, 5S, material flow, ergonomics, and others are necessary considerations for designing a cell for optimal performance. A visual system can be incorporated to convey information and ensure smooth cell operation.
- *Overall machine effectiveness can be improved by adopting setup reduction techniques, utilizing the overall equipment effectiveness metric to monitor machine efficiency, and incorporating a total productive maintenance program to improve machine performance and mitigate potential equipment issues.*
- *As the cell becomes process operational and the process execution matures, enablers like mistake-proofing and materials management can be utilized to fine-tune the process for improved operation.*
- *Due to the inherent variation that exists in processes for establishing optimal flow, Kanbans can be employed for both material replenishment and in-process product movement.* However, the use of Kanbans is

most effective after the establishment of process fundamentals such as standard work, 5S, ergonomics, and cell design.
- *Knowledge management practices, through improvements in information systems coupled with mentoring and training programs that encourage employee learning, are key enablers to ensure that the workforce is capable to not only meet business needs, but also embrace the spirit for continuous improvement.*

13.3 Lean Principles

The Lean methodology strives to improve the business relationship by enabling companies to achieve their operational goals while maximizing value to the customer. The key tenets of Lean, focused on customer value, flow, and waste elimination, can be summarized in five core principles. These principles, which embody the philosophy of Lean, are illustrated in Figure 13.1 and further explained individually (Womack and Jones 1996, p. 16).

1. *Specify value in the eyes of the customer*: Companies exist to provide the goods and services that customers want. Customer value, expressed in terms of a want or need, is fulfilled upon the delivery of the product or service that satisfies the want or need. It is for this reason that the value stream essentially starts and ends with the customer. Value, expressed in terms of the customer, is the starting point, and hence the first principle, for describing Lean.
2. *Identify the value stream and eliminate waste*: The ability to recognize, and document the value stream is the key for identifying wasteful activities that represent opportunities for elimination. Armed with three criteria that define value-added activities, we can identify these areas for potential improvement. Quite simply, the value stream cannot be improved unless its current condition is recognized and fundamentally understood.
3. *Make value flow at the pull of the customer*: From the company's perspective, achieving flow is the capstone activity for operational success. It signifies that the company has successfully implemented Lean fundamentals, which represent the prerequisites, to establishing flow. The ability to *pull* the product through the value stream implies that capacity

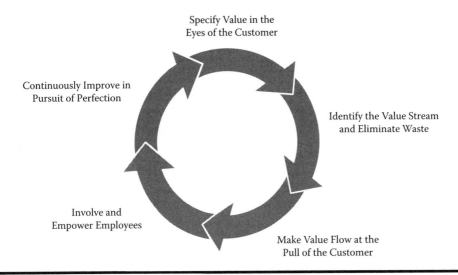

Figure 13.1 Lean principles.

exists in the value stream, and mechanisms are in place to ensure efficient processing.

4. *Involve and empower employees*: Employees are the true lifeblood of the company. Companies that are the most successful in implementing Lean recognize that the expertise of employees is the most critical resource for obtaining real and sustained improvement. Nurturing a culture that encourages employee involvement is the secret to this success.
5. *Continuously improve in pursuit of perfection*: The logical progression of the principles is depicted in Figure 13.1. As illustrated by the figure, this last principle for continuous improvement completes the circle. Those that embrace Lean know that is it not merely an initiative but also a way to run the business. It truly is a never-ending journey.

Appendix A: Using Six Sigma to Improve Product Quality

How can Six Sigma improve product quality? The key is to reduce variation and eliminate defects. Let's explore the basics of Six Sigma to understand how this is accomplished.

The term *sigma* refers to standard deviation, which is a measure of the variation or scatter in a process. Within business and industry, the sigma value is a metric that indicates how well a process is performing, compared to the benchmark value of Six Sigma. Sigma measures the capability of a process to perform defect-free work. A defect is *anything* that may result in customer dissatisfaction.

The common measurement for Six Sigma is defects per unit, where a unit can be virtually anything: a component, an administrative form, a piece of material, a line of software code, and so on. The sigma value is a quality measurement that indicates how often a defect is likely to occur. The higher the sigma value, the less likely that a process will produce defects. As sigma increases, so too does customer satisfaction, while cycle time and cost decrease.

So what does it mean to be Six Sigma? Consider a process that produces one million parts. For this process to meet a Six Sigma quality level, it must produce less than four defective parts (the actual number is 3.4) out of the million that are produced. Clearly, achieving a Six Sigma quality level represents world-class status.

Let's further examine the impact of variation on product quality. Referring to Figure A.1, the variation of two products is depicted and represented by the bell-shaped curves. The product produced using Six Sigma methodologies is shown with less variation, represented by the steeper slope of the curve and more narrow spread around the mean value, than the traditional product.

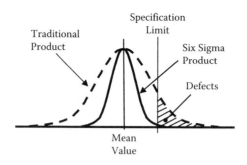

Figure A.1 Product quality comparison.

With the customer specification limit superimposed on the curves, you can see that the shaded area under the curves on the right-hand side of the specification limit line is considerably smaller for the Six Sigma product than for the traditional product. This area corresponds to the quantity of defects that are produced for each product.

Clearly, a Six Sigma product produces far fewer defects translating into less scrap and rework costs. As a result of this reduced variation, Six Sigma methodologies often lead to the identification of product development best practices. Ultimately, exploiting these practices results in the creation of superior products.

As you can see, variation has a significant impact on product quality. Controlling variation leads to improved productivity and lower costs, which translate into a competitive advantage.

Appendix B: Forms and Worksheets

B.1 Baseline Charter Form

Baseline Charter

Event Title:

Problem Statement:

Scope:

Goals/Objectives:

Deliverables:

Schedule/Milestones:

Team Members/Sponsor:

B.2 A3 Project Template

Insert Project Title Here Date: _____

Problem/Background	Future State

Current State	Implementation Plan
	Task | Who | When

Goal	Follow-Up Actions

Root Cause Analysis	

B.3 Baseline Event Planning Checklist

Baseline Event Planning Checklist

- ☐ Identify issue/problem/opportunity for improvement
- ☐ Define the scope, goals, and objectives for the event
- ☐ Select event sponsor
- ☐ Choose baseline event facilitator
- ☐ Select team leader, if appropriate
- ☐ Identify and recruit event participants with concurrence from their management/department
- ☐ Complete baseline charter document
- ☐ Review charter with event sponsor for concurrence and solicit additional approvals as necessary
- ☐ Complete event logistics (event dates, time, location)
- ☐ Prepare and conduct an event kick-off meeting to inform participants of objectives, agenda and schedule
- ☐ Secure funding for conducting event, if necessary
- ☐ Complete travel arrangements for participants, if required
- ☐ Reserve room(s) for event; send event invitation(s) as required
- ☐ Secure materials (notecards, markers, poster-size copy of process map, etc.) for event
- ☐ Schedule debrief session at the end of the baseline event
- ☐ Invite sponsor, stakeholders, and interested parties to the debrief session
- ☐ Define pre-work (include survey of broader audience, if appropriate)
- ☐ Conduct pre-event session(s) to assign and complete pre-work (process maps, data gathering, metrics collection)
- ☐ Acquire any necessary documents prior to the day of the event
- ☐ Conduct event
- ☐ Publish report summarizing results from event

Notes: _____

_____

_____

B.4 Product Analysis Worksheet

PRODUCT ANALYSIS WORKSHEET

Part Name: _____ Date: _____ Time Units: _____

Part Number: _____ Prepared By: _____ Distance Units: _____

Process Step Description	Value-Added Time	Non-Value-Added Time							Notes
	Processing Time	Transportation		Storage/Queue Time				Inspection Time	
		Time	Distance	Raw Material	Between Process	End of Process	Finished Goods		

Total Time

B.5 Operator Analysis Worksheet

OPERATOR ANALYSIS WORKSHEET

Part Name: _____ Date: _____ Time Units: _____
Part Number: _____ Department/Functional Area: _____
Operator: _____ Prepared By: _____

OPERATION		ANALYSIS OF TIME								ASSESSMENT OF TIME		
Step No.	Task Description	Time Duration	Value-Added	Tool-Related	Manual Operation	Material Handling	Walking	Change-Over	Other	Eliminate	Improve/Reduce	Leave As Is	Notes

Total Time

Value-Added = Activities that physically alter the product
Tool-Related = Activities associated with acquiring and using tools
Manual Operation = Processing activities that are not value-added
Material Handling = Activities associated with moving and packaging the product
Walking = Operator movements to acquire parts, tools, etc.
Change-over = Workstation setup and change-over for different products

B.6 Multi-Cycle Analysis Worksheet

Process: _____ Date: _____
Operator: _____ Observer: _____

No.	Operation Description	Work Type	\multicolumn{10}{c	}{Individual Time Measurements (Cycles)}	Total Time	Average Time	Range (High-Low)	Standard Deviation
			1	2	3	4	5	6	7	8	9	10				
		Manual														
		Machine														
		Manual														
		Machine														
		Manual														
		Machine														
		Manual														
		Machine														
		Manual														
		Machine														
		Manual														
		Machine														
		Manual														
		Machine														
		Manual														
		Machine														
		Manual														
		Machine														

B.7 Machine Analysis Worksheet

MACHINE ANALYSIS WORKSHEET

Part Name: _____ Date: _____ Time Units: _____
Part Number: _____ Department/Functional Area: _____
Machine: _____ Prepared By: _____

OPERATION			ANALYSIS OF TIME								ASSESSMENT OF TIME			
Step No.	Task Description	Time Duration	Manual Run	Auto Run	Setup	Tool Change	Load	Unload	Idle/Wait	Clean	Eliminate	Improve/Reduce	Leave As Is	Notes

Total Time

B.8 Standard Work Combination Chart

Standard Work Combination Chart			Plant/Facility:	Date:	Manual Time & Walk Time	
^^^			Value Stream:	Created By:	^^^	
^^^			Product:	Approved By:	Machine Time	
^^^			Shift:	Page: of	^^^	
Step #	Process Step Description	Manual Time	Machine Time	Walk Time	Time Graph	
	Totals					

B.9 Standard Work Chart

Standard Work Chart	Plant/Facility:			Date		Production Volume:
	Value Stream:			Created By:		
	Product:			Approved By:		Takt Time:
	Shift:			Page: of		
Step #	Process Step Description	Manual Time	Machine Time	Walk Time		
	Totals					

B.10 Setup Time Analysis Worksheet

SETUP TIME ANALYSIS WORKSHEET

Part Name: _____ Date: _____ Time Units: _____
Part Number: _____ Department/Functional Area: _____
Machine: _____ Prepared By: _____

OPERATION		ANALYSIS OF TIME		ASSESSMENT OF TIME			
Step No.	Task Description	Time Duration	Internal Setup Time	External Setup Time	Eliminate	Reduce Internal Time	Move to External Time	Notes

Total Time

Appendix C: Glossary

Baseline charter: a document that outlines the team members, scope, and objectives that are required for supporting a baseline event.
Baseline event: a comprehensive, team-based analysis to assess the current state of a process. The objectives of the baseline event are to identify where problems exist, shape a vision for the future, determine where to start and what to do, and solicit management commitment to proceed with an improvement plan.
Bottleneck: an impediment to flow. A condition resulting in a process when the incoming work level into a process step exceeds the output level, resulting in stagnation in product movement through the value stream.
Cell: the co-location of dedicated resources, material, and equipment that are required to manufacture a product or a grouping of similar products.
Cycle time: the total time to complete one part for one process step.
Design for Six Sigma: a methodology to manage and reduce variation in the product design process while meeting all customer expectations and producing products at Six Sigma–quality levels.
Five S (5S): a methodology to transform and maintain a work environment that supports Lean implementation and to promote a culture of discipline and efficiency in the workplace. The term 5S is derived from Japanese words meaning sort, store, shine, standardize, and sustain.
Flow: the continuous movement of products and information through a value stream.
Group technology: a concept for assessing the level of commonality for a collection of parts or products.
Hidden factory: a term that is used to identify the actions and activities that are actually taking place in a process, as opposed to documented work instructions that do not represent nor reflect these activities.

Kanban: a Japanese term that means *signboard*. Within the Lean approach, a Kanban is used as a signal to support the flow of products through the value stream. There are two types of Kanbans: (1) a material Kanban and (2) a production (or in-process) Kanban.

Knowledge management: a system consisting of processes, human behaviors, and tools that enable individuals to access the right information, at a time when it is needed, in order to make the right business decisions.

Lean: a philosophy of producing what is needed, when it is needed, with the minimum amount of time, resources, and space.

Line balancing: the equal distribution of work content across all operators in a process. Line balancing is a requirement for establishing flow.

Little's law: states that the average number of customers in a system (over some interval) is equal to their average arrival rate, multiplied by their average time in the system. In a Lean system, this correlates to the variables of average work in process, throughput, and queue time.

Load chart: a bar chart–type tool that is used to display the distribution of work content by operator.

Mistake-proofing: a Lean philosophy for utilizing the methods and devices for reducing product defects.

Multi-cycle analysis: a time study to assess operator performance. The goal of a multi-cycle analysis is to assess process variability as a precursor to establishing standard work.

Non-value-added activity: an activity that does not meet all three criteria that define a value-added activity. A non-value-added activity utilizes time or resources but does not meet the customer requirements.

Overall equipment effectiveness (OEE): a metric that is based on the characteristics of availability, performance, and quality. The OEE is used most often for a machine analysis, but the OEE calculation can also be utilized to measure cell or department activities.

Product–process matrix: a spreadsheet-type tool that is used to assess the level of commonality across a group of products. This analysis is often performed as part of a cell design for determining which parts will be manufactured within a particular cell.

Pull systems: a manufacturing approach that produces products in direct response to customer orders.

Push systems: a manufacturing approach that relies on forecasts and estimates for pre-determining the quantity of the product to be produced.

Single-minute exchange of die: a Lean concept for reducing the setup time that is associated with a process.
Six Sigma: a statistics-based methodology that is focused on variation reduction and process control.
Spaghetti diagram: a tool that documents the travel paths of a product through the factory.
Standard deviation: the mathematical calculation to quantify the variability for a data set. From a Lean perspective, the standard deviation is calculated as part of a multi-cycle analysis.
Standard work: prescribed work tasks that are performed by workers in a process in order to achieve a linear output rate that matches takt time. Recognized as the "single best way" to perform a task or activity.
Standard work chart: a graphical layout depicting the operation of a cell. Included is a summary of the key process activities along with the walk paths of the operators who are involved in the process.
Standard work combination chart: a tool that displays the combination of manual work time, walk time, and machine processing time for each operation. It is an excellent resource for refining a process design in order to meet the takt time requirements.
Takt time: the term defining the rate of production or the pace of the process output. Mathematically, takt time is expressed as the available work time divided by the customer demand for a given time period.
Theory of constraints: a theory that contends that the overall output of any process is limited, or constrained, by the least productive step in the process.
Throughput time: the total time that it takes the entire process to complete one unit of a product or service.
Time-value chart: a tool that provides a graphical assessment of value-added and non-value-added time in a process.
Total productive maintenance: a management philosophy to proactively maintain machines and equipment in proper working order to minimize downtime and meet the production goals of a Lean enterprise.
Value-added activity: an activity that changes the form, fit, or function of the material or information; is done correctly the first time; and is something that the customers are willing to pay for. All three criteria must be met for an activity to be considered value-added.
Value stream: the sum of all the activities, materials, people, and information that must flow and come together to provide and deliver value to the customers.

Value stream map: a tool that takes a macro-level view of a process and documents the value stream. A key objective of this tool is to aid in identifying areas of waste that represent improvement opportunities.

Visual system: a suite of devices that are designed to share information at a glance.

Waste: a term that is associated with non-value-added activities. Under the Lean philosophy, waste can be grouped into seven different categories (defects, overproduction, inventory, motion, processing, transportation, and waiting) that are known by the acronym DOTWIMP.

Appendix D: Answers

Chapter 1

1. Lean projects tend to be process-centric with emphasis placed on examining value streams and work processes. Six Sigma projects tend to be product-centric, which is focused on variation reduction and process control.
2. Quality levels are highly variable, in low production quantities, with little inventory.
3. Dramatic reductions in product cost, improved quality that enabled interchangeable parts, and increased worker wages.
4. Worker stress, boredom from performing the same repetitive tasks day in and day out, and operator safety.
5. Make each process as efficient and effective as possible, and connect those processes in a stream or continuous chain focused on flow and maximizing customer value.
6. Producing what is needed, when it is needed, with the minimum amount of materials, equipment, labor, and space.
7. The continuous movement of products and information through various processes to create a product.
8. (1) The customer must be willing to pay for the activity, (2) the part or object must change (Note: for nonfactory processes, the second criterion is that the activity must add to the company's knowledge base), and (3) it must be done right the first time.
9. The customer's perspective.

10. Defects, overproduction, transportation, waiting (product), inventory, motion (operator), processing (unnecessary process steps); DOTWIMP.
11. Less than 10%.
12. In a push system, a pre-determined quantity of work is scheduled into the production process. This work quantity is often derived from sales estimates and forecasts. In a pull system, the value stream is engaged in direct response to customer demand. Materials to be used in the process are staged at the point of consumption.

Chapter 2

1. All of the activities, materials, people, and information that must flow and come together to provide and deliver value (product or service) that the customer seeks.
2. The customer.
3. To assess the current state of performance and identify opportunities for improvement.
4. The actions and activities for what is actually taking place in a process, as opposed to documented work instructions that do not represent reality.
5. Between 4 and 10 steps.
6. High-level or macro-level view.
7. 16.5 minutes.
8. 35.5 minutes.
9. Two.
10. 12 minutes.
11. 71.2 minutes.
12. 3T.

Chapter 3

1. A rigorous, team-based analysis to assess the current state of a process. It includes consideration of a future, improved state for the process and the development of a plan to achieve it.
2. To promote "out-of-the-box" thinking. Ideas are generated by participants with no restrictions on cost, resources, or available time.

3. (1) Secure management/leadership support, (2) recruit team members with the right skill-sets, and (3) develop a baseline charter.
4. To outline top-level performance goals required by the process, communicate and advocate the need for conducting the event, and coordinate the recruitment of resources to participate and support the baseline activity.
5. (1) Provides everyone involved with the baseline effort a clear understanding of the focus and direction for the event and (2) serves as a vehicle for communicating and educating others in the organization about the assessment activity.
6. A SMART goal is specific, measurable, achievable, relevant, and time bound.
7. To identify the hand-offs among the process participants.
8. To identify the sources of variation in the process.
9. The 6 Ms represent elements that contribute to variation in a process. They denote categories, all beginning with the letter "M."
10. An A3 template is a structured problem-solving tool that documents a project on a one-page report. The name A3 is derived from the size of the paper of the template.

Chapter 4

1. To document firsthand observations of specific product activities and identify opportunities for improvement.
2. It provides the opportunity to fill out the product analysis worksheet at a later time. It also gives the added benefit of having a permanent record for future analysis and reference.
3. To graphically represent value-added and non-value-added activities within a process.
4. The thickness of the activity line corresponds to the relative time required to complete the task.
5. A graphic-based tool that is used to depict the travel paths of a product through a factory and to document the location and amount of work-inprocess inventory.
6. *White space* refers to the queue time on a time-value chart.
7. 25%.
8. Due to the graphical nature of the tools, they provide an effective and succinct way to communicate to managers and leadership teams. Also,

they are used for displaying results and improvements of a project by displaying "before" and "after" versions.

Chapter 5

1. Takt time refers to the "drumbeat" or "heartbeat" of the production process. It is the rate at which finished products need to be completed in order to meet customer demand.
2. 6 minutes per unit.
3. 375 units.
4. The takt time is doubled.
5. 2.5 minutes per unit.
6. 5 operators. (The calculated staffing requirement is 4.8 but rounded up.)
7. 2.75 minutes per unit.
8. A load chart is a simple bar chart displaying the work content by operator. By superimposing the takt time requirement on the chart, flow is established by balancing the work content among all operators with each operator's work content equal to or below the takt time value.
9. A bottleneck is a condition where the input level entering a process activity exceeds the output level causing a buildup of input and ultimately results in stagnation of the product in the value stream.
10. A multi-cycle analysis is an operator time study to assess operator variability. Multiple cycles of an operator performing a work task are timed with the data captured and cataloged on a worksheet. Calculations are performed to derive the average, or mean value of the data set, and the standard deviation.

Chapter 6

1. The OEE is an aggregate, calculated metric to assess machine effectiveness. It is based on the factors of machine availability, performance, and quality.
2. 93%.
3. 85%.
4. 405 minutes.

5. 365 minutes.
6. 90%.
7. 51%.
8. 45%.

Chapter 7

1. To transform and maintain a clean and safe work environment that supports Lean implementation.
2. Five S can be applied in every environment, both factory and non-factory. It also can be applied to software and computer files.
3. To ensure there are consistent and repeatable practices in place for executing the first 3 Ss.
4. Promoting a culture of order and efficiency in the workplace and raising employee morale. Clean work environments gain credibility with customers, suppliers, and visitors to the company.
5. Sustain; it requires a robust operating system and the discipline for the system to be maintained.
6. Participation of all team members in the work area, defined roles and responsibilities that are understood by everyone, designated times for 5S and an operating system that is consistently followed.
7. Five S can be implemented anytime. However, due to its ease of implementation, it is often used as the starting point for launching Lean improvement.
8. Visual cues convey information to employees in the work area regarding the storage and placement of items.

Chapter 8

1. Standard work defines a consistent, and agreed-upon, best way to perform a specified task with the goal of repeatability and high quality.
2. Tasks should be fairly repetitive; they should be capable of being performed by an average person on an average day; the importance of standard work should be recognized and owned by all parties involved in the activity.

3. To first eliminate and minimize non-value-added activities, and then to establish standard work for the remaining work activities needed for the process.
4. Three machines. (The calculated value of 2.875 is rounded up to 3.)
5. To display the manual work time, walk time, and machine processing time for each operation in a production sequence.
6. Standard work chart.
7. Due to changes in customer demand, takt time, or staffing requirement. Changes to any of these factors will require adjustments to standard work.

Chapter 9

1. A cell is a grouping of people, workstations, machines, and equipment dedicated to producing a designated group of products.
2. To increase flexibility for producing a high variety of products in small batch sizes while concurrently maintaining the productivity benefits attributed to large-scale production.
3. Proximity to docks, material feeder and storage locations, and special processing facilities.
4. Equipment access for maintenance and repair, materials flow, tool storage, operator safety, travel paths, ergonomic issues that are related to workstation design, and worker communication, among others.
5. It conveys information to workers at a glance and helps ensure the successful operation of the cell.
6. *Visual displays*—provide data and information; *visual controls*—guide the actions of people.
7. A concept of assessing the level of commonality for a collection of parts or products.
8. A spreadsheet-type tool that aids in determining the level of commonality for a group of products.

Chapter 10

1. Smaller setup time allows for smaller batch sizes, frees capacity, improves scheduling and flexibility, and reduces inventory and lead

time, thereby enabling production to be more responsive and more closely reflect true customer demand.
2. *Internal setup time*—the machine must be stopped to perform the action; *external setup time*—the action can be performed while the machine is running.
3. The goal is to maximize external setup time and reduce internal setup time.
4. TPM is a proactive approach to maximize the operational effectiveness of machines and equipment by ensuring that machines suffer no breakdowns, are not subjected to small stops and slow running, and produce no defects, all while maintaining safe operation with no accidents.
5. Since Lean processes typically have low inventory levels, any equipment failure can have an immediate and significant impact in meeting takt time and the production schedule.
6. By taking over repetitive tasks or actions that depend on memory or vigilance, workers are free to pursue more value-added activities.
7. Prevention identifies that a defect is about to occur, and detection identifies that a defect has occurred. From a business perspective, it is certainly preferable to avoid producing defects, as opposed to creating defects that need to be scrapped or reworked.
8. Counting and grouping methods, motion-step or sequencing methods, and physical or contact methods.

Chapter 11

1. Inventory levels and lead times increase, and available floor space is reduced due to the need to support higher levels of WIP inventory.
2. Offer discounts during low-demand periods or renegotiate delivery schedules with existing customers.
3. Hire more workers or increase available working time (overtime).
4. Takt time decreases by half.
5. To replenish material consumed by the production process (material Kanbans) and to pace the movement of products in a process to ensure flow (production Kanbans).
6. Mismatched cycle times, large transportation distance, and long lead times or process instability.

7. Quality levels of both the product and process are stable, demand variability is understood, customer and supplier relationships are established, processes are documented, and standard work is used.
8. 240 units per day.

Chapter 12

1. The thing going through an administrative process is not a physical product, but rather information that cannot be directly seen or tracked.
2. Raw data, company knowledge and intellectual property, and employee expertise.
3. A system consisting of processes, human behaviors, and tools that enable individuals to access the right information, at a time when it is needed, in order to make the right business decisions.
4. Explicit knowledge is data that can be communicated, documented, and stored in computer systems; tacit knowledge is knowledge that resides in people's minds. It is the expertise, judgment, skills, experience, tribal knowledge, awareness, and wisdom that each person possesses.
5. Explicit knowledge can be enhanced with improvements in processes and information systems with readily accessible data; tacit knowledge can be addressed with training, pilot programs for new hires, and mentoring programs, among others.

References

Black, J. Temple, and Steve L. Hunter. 2003. *Lean Manufacturing Systems and Cell Design*. Dearborn, MI: Society of Manufacturing Engineers, pp. 59, 210, 258.

Collison, Chris, and Geoff Parcell. 2004. *Learning to Fly*. West Sussex, UK: Capstone, p. 18.

Domm, Robert W. 2009. *Michigan Yesterday & Today*. Minneapolis, MN: MBI Pub. Co. LLC and Voyageur Press, pp. 28–30.

Fiore, Clifford. 2005. Conducting a baseline assessment. In *Accelerated Product Development: Combining Lean and Six Sigma for Peak Performance*. New York: Productivity Press, pp. 47–66.

George, Michael L. 2002. *Lean Six Sigma: Combining Six Sigma Quality with Lean Speed*. New York: McGraw-Hill, pp. 93–94.

George, Michael L., David Rowlands, Mark Price, and John Maxey. 2005. *The Lean Six Sigma Pocket Toolbook*. New York: McGraw-Hill Education, pp. 33–54, 202.

Goldratt, Eliyahu M., and Jeff Cox. 1992. *The Goal: A Process of Ongoing Improvement*. Great Barrington, MA: North River Press.

Hyer, Nancy Lea, and Urban Wemmerlöv. 2002. *Reorganizing the Factory: Competing through Cellular Manufacturing*. Portland, OR: Productivity Press, pp. 99, 164.

Krafcik, John F. 1988. Triumph of the Lean production system. *Sloan Management Review* Fall: pp. 41–52.

Lean. 2007. *Merriam-Webster's Collegiate Dictionary*, 11th ed. Springfield, MA: Merriam-Webster, Incorporated.

Little, John D. C. 1961. Little's law as viewed on its 50th anniversary (PDF). *Operations Research* 59 (3): 536–549.

Nihon Puranto Mentenansu Kyōkai. 1996. *TPM for Every Operator*. Portland, OR: Productivity Press, p. 30.

Ohno, Taiichi. 1988. *Toyota Production System: Beyond Large-Scale Production*. Portland, OR: Productivity Press, p. 129.

Rother, Mike, and John Shook. 2003. *Learning to See: Value Stream Mapping to Create Value and Eliminate MUDA*. Brookline, MA: Lean Enterprise Institute.

Rubin, Melanie, and Hiroyuki Hirano. 1996. *5S for Operators: 5 Pillars of the Visual Workplace*. Portland, OR: Productivity Press, pp. 11–27.

Sekine, Ken'ichi, and Keisuke Arai. 1998. *TPM for the Lean Factory: Innovative Methods and Worksheets for Equipment Management.* Portland, OR: Productivity Press, pp. 2–10, 189.

Shingo, Shigeo. 1985. *A Revolution of Manufacturing: The SMED System.* Cambridge, MA: Productivity Press, pp. 22–25.

Shingo, Shigeo. 1986. *Zero Quality Control: Source Inspection and the Poka-Yoke System.* Cambridge, MA: Productivity Press, pp. 99–133.

Spear, Steven, and H. Kent Bowen. 1999. Decoding the DNA of the Toyota Production System. *Harvard Business Review* 77, no. 5 (September–October): 96–106.

Wilson, Lonnie. 2010. *How to Implement Lean Manufacturing.* New York: McGraw-Hill Professional, pp. 138–141, 176, 416.

Womack, James P., and Daniel T. Jones. 1996. *Lean Thinking: Banish Waste and Create Wealth in Your Corporation.* New York: Simon & Schuster, pp. 16–26.

Index

This index covers the preface and appendixes. Page numbers with f and n refer to figures and footnotes, respectively.

A

A3 project, 39, 40f, 111f
Activities
    non-value-added; *see also* Waste
        criteria, 7
        definition, 122
        examples, 7
        Lean and, 3
        tools in highlighting, *see* Spaghetti diagram; Time-value charts
        in typical value stream, 8
    value-added
        criteria, 7
        definition, 123
        Lean guidelines, 103
        tools in highlighting, *see* Spaghetti diagram; Time-value charts
        in typical value stream, 8
Administrative processes, 4n, 16, 97
Andon lights, 81
Answers to questions, 125–132
    Chapter 1: Lean fundamentals, 125–126
    Chapter 2: value streams and value stream mapping, 126
    Chapter 3: Lean baseline assessment, 126–127
    Chapter 4: product analysis, 127–128
    Chapter 5: operator analysis, 128
    Chapter 6: machine analysis, 128–129
    Chapter 7: five S, 129
    Chapter 8: standard work, 129–130
    Chapter 9: cell design, 130
    Chapter 10: process improvement enablers, 130–131
    Chapter 11: materials management, 131–132
    Chapter 12: knowledge management, 132
Assessment debriefing, 39
Autonomous maintenance, 88
Availability, 61, 62, 63

B

Baseline charter, 25–26, 27f, 110f, 121
Baseline event, 24–25, 39, 112f, 121
Basic process map, 22, 29, 30f
Bottlenecks, 53, 97, 121

C

Cell, 79, 80f, 121; *see also* Cell design
Cell design, 79–83
    answers to questions, 130
    cell definition, 79–80
    group technology, 81–82
    Lean guidelines, 103
    questions, 83
    requirement, 79, 80
    visual systems, 80–81
Cellular model, 79
Champion, *see* Management sponsor

135

Changeover (C/O) time, 13f, 14
Charts, 81; *see also* Load charts; Standard work charts; Standard work combination charts; Time-value charts
C/O, *see* Changeover (C/O) time
Constraints, theory of, 53, 123; *see also* Garden hose analogy
Contact method, 89
Costs, 3, 4, 108
Counting and grouping methods, 89
Culture, 102–103, 105
Current state, definition, 21–22, 22f, 28–35
Customer demand, 9, 51, 74, 86
Customers, 14f, 94
Customer satisfaction, 107
Customer value, 7, 8, 104; *see also* Activities
Cycle times
  definition, 121
  as improvement opportunities, 3
  Lean and, 4
  mismatched, 93
  in operator process variation, 57
  in value stream map, 13f, 14

D

Data, 4, 14f, 98
Defects
  definition, 107
  Kanban rule, 94
  mistake-proofing solutions, 89, 89n
  product quality and, 108f
  as waste category, 8
Deliverables, 26, 27
Detailed process map, 32–35, 33f
Diamond symbol, 29
DOTWIMP, 8, 124; *see also* Waste

E

Early equipment management, 88
Education and training, 88
Electronic flow, 14f
Employee involvement, 105
Employees, 102, 105
Environment
  in ergonomics, 58
  in five S, 67, 68, 69
  as input, 32
  team, 36
  as TPM pillar, 88
Ergonomics, 58, 79, 103
Explicit knowledge, 98, 99
External setup time, 86

F

5S, *see* Five S (5S)
Facilitators, 28
Factory processes, 15, 98f
Finished goods symbol, 14f
Firsthand observation, 11, 15, 86
Five S (5S), 67–70
  answers to questions, 129
  definition, 67, 121
  Lean guidelines, 103
  questions, 70
  shine phase, 68, 69
  significance, 70
  sort, 67, 68, 69
  standardize phase, 68, 69
  store phase, 67, 69
  sustain phase, 68, 70
  transformation and, 103
Floor lines, 81
Flow, 7, 104, 121
Focused improvement, 88
Ford, Henry, 5–6
Forms and worksheets, *see* Worksheets and forms
Four-quadrant model, 23f, 36, 39

G

Garden hose analogy, 53–55
Glossary of terms, 121–124
The Goal: A Process of Ongoing Improvement (1992), 53
Goals, 25, 27
Goldratt, Eliyahu, 53
Grouping methods and counting, 89
Group technology, 81–82, 121

H

Health and safety environment, 88
Hidden factory, 12, 121
Human factors, 56

I

Ideal state, definition, 22f, 22, 36
Improvement opportunities, 3, 11;
    see also Costs; Cycle times;
    Quality
Improvement projects, identification and
    ranking of potential, 22f, 22–23, 36,
    39
Information, 4n, 97, 98f
In-process Kanbans, 93
Inputs
    conventional format, 32f
    definition, 32
    in detailed process map, 33f
    function, 32
    identification, 32, 34–35
Internal setup time, 86
Inventory
    waste, 8
    work-in-process, 9, 46, 91, 94–95

K

Kanbans, 92–94, 122, 103–104
Key issues, identification and ranking
    examples, 35
    flow, 22f
    organizing, 35–36, 37f, 38f
    overview, 22
Knowledge, 98–99; see also Knowledge
    management
Knowledge management, 97–99
    answers to questions, 132
    definition, 98, 122
    Lean guidelines, 104
    questions, 99
    significance, 97
Knowledge management system, 98–99
Krafcik, John, 6

L

Leadership/management support, 24
Lean
    baseline assessment, see Lean baseline
        assessment
    definition, 6, 122
    fundamentals, see Lean fundamentals
    history, 5–6
    implementation, see Lean
        implementation
    key tenets, 7, 104; see also Customer
        value; Flow; Waste
    LeanSigma, 5
    most important virtue, x
    perspective, 101
    principles, 104–105, 105f
    vs. Six Sigma, 3–5
Lean baseline assessment, 21–42
    answers to questions, 126–127
    definition, 21
    execution, 28–41
    key steps, 21–23, 22f
    questions, 42
    significance, 102
    success factors, 23–27
Lean fundamentals, 3–10
    answers to questions, 125–126
    customer value, 7, 8
    flow, 7
    Lean; see also Lean
        definition, 6
        history, 5–6
        vs. Six Sigma, 3–5
    push vs. pull systems, 9–10
    questions, 10
    waste categories, 8–9
Lean implementation, 101–105
    general guidelines, 101–104
    Lean perspective, 101
    Lean principles, 104–105
LeanSigma, 5
*Learning to See: Value Stream Mapping to
    Create Value and Eliminate MUDA*
    (2003), 15
Lights, Andon, 81

Line balancing
  application, 52–53, 55–56
  definition, 122
  standard work and, 72–73
Little, John D.C., 94n
Little's law, 95, 122
Load charts
  definition, 122
  Lean guidelines, 103
  in machine analysis, 73f
  in operator analysis, 52, 52f, 55f
Lead time, 93
Lot quantity, 13, 14

M

Machine analysis, 61–64
  blank worksheets, 116f
  overall equipment effectiveness (OEE), 61–64
  questions, 64
  significance, 61
Machine effectiveness, 103
Machine requirement, 72
Machine run time, 72
Machines, 32, 34f; *see also* Machine analysis
Made-to-order systems, 9
Man, 32, 34, 34f; *see also* Operator analysis
Management/leadership support, 24
Management sponsor, 24, 26, 27
Manual flow symbol, 14f
Massachusetts Institute of Technology, 6
Material flow symbol, 14f
Material Kanbans, 92
Materials, 32, 34f; *see also* Material management
Materials management, 91–95
  answers to questions, 131–132
  Kanbans, 92–94
  Lean guidelines, 103
  Little's law, 94–95
  overview, 91–92
  questions, 95
Mean, 57f, 57, 58
Measurement, 32, 34, 34f
Meetings, 28

Merriam-Webster's Collegiate Dictionary (2007), 6
Method, 32, 34, 34f, 89
Milestones, 26, 27
Mismatched cycle times, 93
Mistake-proofing, 88–89, 89n, 103, 122
Mother Nature, 32; *see also* Environment
Motion, 8
Motion-step method, 89
Multi-cycle analysis, 57–58, 103, 115f, 122

N

Non-factory processes, 4n, 7, 98f
Non-value-added activities; *see also* waste
  criteria, 7
  definition, 122
  examples, 7
  Lean and, 3
  tools in highlighting, *see* Spaghetti diagram; Time-value charts
  in typical value stream, 8
Non-value-added time, 43; *see also* Spaghetti diagrams; Time value charts

O

Objectives, 25, 27
OEE, *see* Overall equipment effectiveness (OEE)
Ohno, Taiichi, 94
Olds, Ransom, 6
Operating time, 62
Operations Research (1961), 94
Operator analysis, 49–59
  answers to questions, 128
  bottlenecks, 53
  efficiency, 49, 51
  ergonomics, 58
  garden hose analogy, 53–55
  line balancing, 52–53, 55–56
  operator process variation, 56–58
  questions, 59
  significance, 49
  takt time, 51–52
  worksheets, 49, 50f, 114f

Operator process variation, 56–58
Operator safety, 79, 103
Operator symbol, 14f
Operator variability, 58
Outputs, 32, 32f
Overall equipment effectiveness (OEE), 61–64
    definition, 122
    elements, 61–63
    Lean guidelines, 103
    significance, 63–64
    TPM and, 88
    value, 63
Overall setup time, 86
Overproduction, 8
Overtime work, 92

P

"Peeling the onion layer by layer" approach, 13
Performance
    identification of current state, 11; *see also* Lean baseline assessment; Value stream mapping
    OEE element, 61, 62, 63
Physical method, 89
Planned maintenance, 88
Planned production time, 62
Planned shift downtime, 62
Post-World War II, 6
Preventive mistake-proofing, 89, 89n
Problem statement, 25, 27
Process-centric process, 4; *see also* Lean
Process improvement, 102
Process improvement enablers, 85–89
    answers to questions, 130–131
    mistake-proofing, 88–89, 89n, 122
    questions, 89
    setup reduction, 85–87
    total productive maintenance (TPM), 87–88
Processing time, 14
Process instability, 93
Process steps, unnecessary (Processing), 8
Process step symbol, 14f

Product analysis, 43–48
    answers to questions, 127–128
    communication with tools, 47–48
    purpose, 43
    questions, 48
    spaghetti diagram, 46–47, 47f
    time-value charts, 45–46, 45f
    worksheets, 43, 44f, 45, 113f
Product-centric process, 4; *see also* Six-Sigma
Production Kanbans, 93, 93f
Productivity and variation, 108
Product–process matrix, 81–82, 82f, 103
Product quality, 107–108, 108f
Products, 98f, 122; *see also* Product analysis
Project plans, selection and development of detailed project, 22f, 23, 39
Pull systems, 9–10, 122
Push systems, 9–10, 122

Q

Quality, 3, 62, 63
Quality leadership, 5
Quality maintenance, 88
Quality management, 5
Questions, asking, x, 28, 102
Questions (end of chapter)
    Chapter 1: Lean fundamentals, 10
    Chapter 2: value streams and value stream mapping, 16–17
    Chapter 3: Lean baseline assessment, 42
    Chapter 4: product analysis, 48
    Chapter 5: operator analysis, 59
    Chapter 6: machine analysis, 64
    Chapter 7: five S, 70
    Chapter 8: standard work, 77
    Chapter 9: cell design, 83
    Chapter 10: process improvement enablers, 89
    Chapter 11: materials management, 95
    Chapter 12: knowledge management, 99
Queue time
    Little law, 94–95
    time value charts, 46, 46n
    value stream map, 14, 15

R

Reactive mistake-proofing, 89, 89n
Rectangle symbol, 29
Red tagging process, 69
Rework cycle, 5
Root cause analysis, 102
Rother, Mike, 15

S

6 Ms (Man, machine, material, method, measurement, mother nature), 32, 34–35, 34f
Safety environment and health, 88
Schedule, 26, 27
Scope, 25, 27
Seiri (Sort), 67, 68, 69
Seiso (Shine), 68, 69
Seiton (Store), 67, 69
Seketsu (Standardize), 68, 69
Sequencing method, 89
Setup reduction, 85–87
Setup time analysis worksheet, 119f
Setup times, 86–87
Shadow boards, 81
Shift length, 62
Shine phase, 68, 69
Shingo, Shigeo, 85, 88
Shitsuke (Sustain), 68, 70
Shook, John, 15
Sigma value, 107
Signs, safety, 81
Single-minute exchange of die (SMED), 85, 123
Six Sigma
  common measurement, 107
  definition, 123
  design for, 121
  to improve product quality, 107–108
  LeanSigma, 5
  primary benefit, 4
  vs. Lean, 3–5
SMART goals, 25
SMED, *see* Single-minute exchange of die (SMED)
Sort, 67, 68, 69
Spaghetti diagram, 46–47
  definition, 46, 123
  example, 47f
  Lean guidelines, 102
  significance, 102
Staffing requirement, 51–52, 103
Standard deviation (σ)
  definition, 123
  functions, 57f, 57–58
  representations, 57n
  sigma and, 107
Standardize phase, 68, 69
Standard work, 71–77
  adjusting, 74, 77f
  answers to questions, 129–130
  criteria to successful, 71
  definition, 71, 123
  goal, 71
  Lean guidelines, 103
  line-balancing and, 72–73
  questions, 77
  tools, *see* Standard work charts; Standard work combination charts
Standard work charts
  blank chart, 118f
  definition, 73, 118f, 123
  example, 76f
  significance, 74
Standard work combination charts
  blank chart, 117f
  definition, 73, 123
  example, 75f
  significance, 74
Store phase, 67, 69
Streamlined process, 103
Suppliers, 14f, 94
Sustain phase, 68, 70
Swim lane maps
  benefit, 29, 32
  definition, 29
  example, 31f

T

Tacit knowledge, 98, 99
Takt, 51
Takt time, 51–52, 71, 103, 123

Task to document reality, 12n
Team composition, 24–25
Team members, 26, 27
Terminator symbol, 29
Throughput time, 14, 123
Time-value charts, 45–46
   definition, 123
   example, 45f
   Lean guidelines, 102
Total productive maintenance (TPM), 87–88, 103, 123
Toyota, 6
Toyota Production System, 94
Training and education, 88
Transactional processes, 97
Transportation, 8; *see also* Cell design
Transportation distance, 93
Truck shipment symbol, 14f

U

Uptime, 13f, 14

V

Value, 11, 104
Value-added activities
   criteria, 7
   definition, 123
   Lean guidelines, 103
   tools in highlighting, *see* Spaghetti diagram; Time-value charts
   in typical value stream, 8
Value-added time, 46; *see also* Spaghetti diagrams; Time-value charts
Value stream map; *see also* Value stream mapping
   definition, 124
   example, 13f
   function, 12, 102
   key benefit, 14–15
   reasons for creation, 11
   significance, 102
   symbols, 14f, 14
Value stream mapping, 11–17; *see also* Value streams; Value stream map
   answers to questions, 126
   defining value stream, 11–12
   definition, 11
   function, 11, 12f
   mapping considerations, 12–15
   process considerations, 15–16
   questions, 16–17
   significance, 11–12
Value streams; *see also* Value stream mapping
   answers to questions, 126
   definition, 11, 123
   engagement approaches, 9–10
   Lean principles, 104
   map, *see* Value stream map
   percentage of activities in typical, 8
Variable demand, 91
Variation, 91, 107–108, 108f
Visual controls, 81
Visual cues, 97
Visual displays, 81
Visual systems, 80–81, 103, 124

W

Waiting waste, 8, 46; *see also* Queue time
Waste; *see also* Non-value-added activities
   categories, 8–9
   definition, 124
   elimination, 103, 104
   examples, 7, 85
   Lean and, 7
   reduction, 103
White space, 46n
Work-in-process (WIP) inventory, 9, 46, 91, 94–95
Worksheets and forms, 109–119
   A3 project template, 111f
   baseline charter form, 110f
   baseline event planning checklist, 112f
   machine analysis worksheet, 116f
   multi-cycle analysis worksheet, 115f
   operator analysis worksheet, 114f
   product analysis worksheet, 113f
   setup time analysis worksheet, 119f
   standard work chart, 118f
   standard work combination chart, 117f

About the Author

Clifford (Cliff) Fiore has been employed by a Fortune 500 company for the past 30 years and is a certified Lean expert and Six Sigma black belt. He holds a bachelor of science degree in mechanical engineering technology and a master of business administration degree in technology management. His early career stops included positions in manufacturing engineering, design engineering, and production support.

For the past 18 years, Cliff has been involved with continuous improvement activities associated with the application of Lean and Six Sigma. He has gained extensive experience in applying these concepts in numerous manufacturing, supply chain, and administrative processes, particularly in the area of product development.

Cliff has authored two previous books on the application of Lean methods in product development: *Lean Strategies for Product Development*, published by American Society for Quality (ASQ) in 2003, and *Accelerated Product Development*, published by Productivity Press in 2004.

Cliff has been an adjunct faculty member in Arizona's Maricopa County Community College District for the past 15 years, teaching courses in Lean manufacturing, blueprint reading, technical writing, and properties of materials.